Praise for *Personal Nonviolence: A Practical Spirituality for Peacemakers*

"Many of us work hard to stop war, injustice and nuclear weapons. We're often not so good at radiating peace to those around us. Gerry Vanderhaar's book will help us all go deeper into the practice of inner nonviolence and personal peace. I hope this book will be read and studied by all Pax Christi groups and members so that together we become better practitioners of personal nonviolence, people who radiate the peace of Christ, and like Gerry Vanderhaar, teachers of peace to a culture of war." – John Dear, Pax Christi USA Ambassador of Peace and author of *The Questions of Jesus, Disarming the Heart, Living Peace*, and *The God of Peace*

"Gerry Vanderhaar's legacy to all of us is an extraordinary book about personal nonviolence. He writes what he came to know and live – that a spirituality of nonviolence will pull our centers of gravity toward community and our broken world, making us 'impatient – angry in the peace of Christ' until the New Creation flowers more fully." – Marie Dennis, Maryknoll Office for Global Concerns and vice-president, Pax Christi International

"This wonderful little book belongs in the library of every peacemaker. It is full of good thoughts and practical wisdom that Gerry gathered over a lifetime of service to the Gospel of Peace. The necessity of personal nonviolence is linked to a Social Gospel that challenges the empire-builder nationalists who continue to crucify Jesus in our own time. These last words are a fitting tribute to a man who did so much for Pax Christi and for the world." – Joe Fahey, Professor of Religious Studies at Manhattan College and longtime friend of Gerry Vanderhaar

"In this perfect primer on nonviolence, Gerry Vanderhaar has also given us the diary of a splendid peacemaker, a man of breathtaking civility, and a dear, missing friend whose sacred sense that 'people really do hunger for decency' convinced us to be hopeful time and again. If we are to face down this present Empire using only the tricks of Jesus, Gandhi, and King, this book, warm with Gerry's love, belongs in our hip pockets." – Molly Fumia, writer and longtime member of Pax Christi USA and friend of Gerry and Janice Vanderhaar. Current member of the Pax Christi USA Anti-Racism Team.

Personal Nonviolence
A Practical Spirituality for Peacemakers

Personal Nonviolence

A Practical Spirituality for Peacemakers

by Dr. Gerard Vanderhaar

WIPF & STOCK · Eugene, Oregon

Wipf and Stock Publishers
199 W 8th Ave, Suite 3
Eugene, OR 97401

Personal Nonviolence
A Practical Spirituality for Peacemakers
By Vanderhaar, Gerard
Copyright©2006 by Vanderhaar, Gerard
ISBN 13: 978-1-4982-3427-6
Publication date 7/14/2015
Previously published by Pax Christi USA, 2006

To all those who have helped and inspired me on my peacemaking journey.

Contents

Foreword

In the book of Proverbs (10:7) we read, "The memory of a good person is a blessing."

The memory of Gerry Vanderhaar is a blessing. I knew this good man as a friend. We drank mint juleps together as we watched the Kentucky Derby. I once stayed with Gerry and his wife, Janice, at their home in Memphis. The three of us stood in shared silence and grief at the motel where Martin Luther King Jr. was gunned down. We walked Beale Street under summer stars in Memphis and celebrated Mardi Gras on Bourbon Street in New Orleans. For many years we were part of the gathering at Bill and Mary Carry's motor home during Pax Christi USA's annual assembly, sharing great conversation and enough laughter to last a lifetime.

The memory of Gerry Vanderhaar is a blessing. I knew this good man as a colleague. We served together for many years on the Pax Christi USA National Council. We co-authored a book for Pax Christi USA, *The Way of Peace*. We piloted an alternative conflict resolution project on the question, "Is competition good or bad for us?" (I know I was for it but can't remember where Gerry stood.) We had many conversations on how Pax Christi USA could impact national policy if enough Christians followed the invitation of Jesus to live nonviolently.

The memory of Gerry Vanderhaar is a blessing. I knew this good man as a peacemaker. Gerry possessed that rare, single-minded passion to an ideal, a pursuit that never wavers, that stays the course in season and out. Gerry's passion was nonviolence and he offered his life to its realization. He was one of the founding members of Pax Christi USA, the national Catholic peace movement, and served many terms on its National Council, twice as its chair. For twenty-eight years Dr. Vanderhaar was a professor of religion and peace studies at Christian Brothers University in Memphis. He started a peace studies minor and was instrumental in establishing the Gandhi Institute there. He was a founder of the MidSouth Peace and Justice Center. Janice and he spent their leisure or vacation time visiting "enemy" countries to build bridges of peace. Gerry lectured on peace and demonstrated for peace and brought countless people together to discuss and pray for peace.

Most of all, Gerry wrote about peace and nonviolence. *Personal Nonviolence: A Practical Spirituality for Nonviolence* is a gourmet taste, a five-star appetizer of Gerry's six books on peace and nonviolence. We need this book now more than ever. What government seriously considers the nonviolent alternative in the midst of national and international crises? Who really believes that nonviolence is an alternative to war, which now claims a 90 percent civilian casualty rate? Why in this war-crazed nation are those who claim to follow the nonviolent Jesus impotent, frightened, silent, or, worse yet, vocal supporters of smart bombs and innocent bloodshed? Is there a nonviolent path to lead us out of our violent inner-city mazes? And how can we form nonviolent hearts wide enough to embrace the enemy, wherever that enemy is?

Gerry of the giant heart and gentle smile, we shall miss you. William James once said of very good people, "It is not possible to be quite as mean as we naturally are, when they have passed before us." My bet is that readers of this book will find themselves a little less enamored with the meanness of violence, a lot more prone to take action for peace. That would make the memory of this good man, Gerard Vanderhaar, a true blessing.

Mary Lou Kownacki, OSB
November 2005

Introduction

"I plan to stand by nonviolence," said the Reverend Dr. Martin Luther King Jr., shortly before he was killed, "because I have found it to be a philosophy of life that regulates not only my dealings in the struggle for racial justice but also my dealings with people and with my own self."

Much has been written about nonviolence in the struggle for racial justice. Not nearly so much has been written about nonviolence toward other people and toward one's self. This book is about that kind of personal nonviolence, in the context of a spirituality that is practical for our time.

A realistic spirituality for Christian peacemakers, as we focus on nonviolence toward other people and toward ourselves, can never ignore the bigger picture. Karl Barth liked to say that theology should be done with the Bible in one hand and the daily newspaper in the other. As we attempt to act nonviolently amidst the ever-present pressures from the Principalities and Powers (as the Epistles of Paul call them) of our age, we need a reliable compass pointing in the direction of soul stability.

Such a spirituality is based on Biblical wisdom and Christian tradition, grounded in the life and teachings of Jesus Christ. These teachings can best guide contemporary peacemakers, I am convinced, when they are filtered through the active nonviolence gifted to the world by people such as Mohandas Gandhi and Martin Luther King Jr. In this kind of nonviolence the personal and the political come together.

Part One

Getting Started

Two of the twentieth century's prophets of nonviolence, Mohandas Gandhi and Martin Luther King Jr., opened up a new range of possibilities for calm, courageous, and effective action. Their strong, active nonviolence can influence our personal lives very deeply. It can shape what we say, what we do, how we think. It can provide a practical spirituality for our lives. We may not do great deeds, move mountains, or change the world, but the nonviolent way we meet the multiple challenges we confront every day can make a great difference in our lives and in the lives of those around us.

Chapter 1

My Journey to Nonviolence

Youthful Ideals

My journey toward a practical, realistic spirituality began in the early 1960s. I had entered the novitiate of the Dominican Order in 1950, was ordained a priest in 1957, and taught philosophy and theology in Catholic colleges. As a young Dominican priest-teacher I considered myself alive to the world of my students. I tried to be immersed in the traditional Catholic spirituality of the time, attempting to understand and conform to the will of God.

The decade of the 1960s started off on a rousing note. John Kennedy was elected President, the first Catholic to hold the office. He challenged millions of us to look outward. "Ask not what your country can do for you; ask what you can do for your country." And, many of us would add, "and what we can do for the world." My vision turned more and more outward. Suddenly everything worthwhile seemed possible.

My awareness took a quantum leap in 1962, when I was sent to Rome and the Second Vatican Council began. Genial Pope John XXIII had opened windows, and lots of fresh air was pouring in. Pope John received Khrushchev's son-in-law in the Vatican. I was there in Rome when this representative from "godless" communism was welcomed in the heart of the Catholic Church. Something new and important was stirring. My increasing involvement in the unfolding spirit of Vatican II led me to a greater concentration on the problems of this world rather than the rewards of the next.

I listened anew to Martin Luther King Jr. and the civil rights movement back home. I applauded him.

With 1963's Easter sunshine Pope John gave us *Pacem in Terris* and called us forth with renewed hopes for peace. I had become hooked by the spirit of Vatican II that would be expressed in the opening words of its Pastoral Constitution on the Church in the Modern World (*Gaudium et Spes*): "The joys and the hopes, the griefs and the anxieties of the [people] of this age, especially those who are poor or in any way afflicted, these are the joys and hopes, the griefs and anxieties of the followers of Christ."

Harsher Reality

Then, just as suddenly, the skies darkened. Pope John died that summer of 1963. Civil rights workers were murdered in Mississippi and assaulted and threatened across the South. President Kennedy was assassinated in November. I had visited the former Nazi concentration camp at Dachau, had seen how far human cruelty could go, and begun to realize that modern warfare had locked in a similar cruelty with its awesome nuclear weapons. The United States and the Soviet Union had developed intercontinental missiles to carry hydrogen bombs to each other's heartlands, capable of incinerating millions who were as innocent as the inmates of Dachau.

Another disturbing picture, of Buddhist monks immolating themselves on the streets of Saigon in Vietnam, lingered in my memory. Like others, I was beginning to glimpse the dark side of Camelot, the early 1960s slide into the quagmire of U.S. involvement in Southeast Asia.

Vietnam. For me and many others, it dominated the rest of the decade. The Second Vatican Council ended in 1965 with the somber warning to evaluate war with an entirely new attitude. But in the jungles of Southeast Asia, and in the offices of the Pentagon, war was being prosecuted with the same old ugly attitudes: identify the enemy, overwhelm with superior force, kill as many as possible with ever-more deadly weapons.

I, like many others, watched, first in dismay and then in anger, as grim GIs torched huts with cigarette lighters, as screaming jets dumped napalm on rice paddies, as clattering helicopters sprayed indiscriminate death. I, like many others, also watched, at first in dismay and then in anger, the tightlipped attempts by President Lyndon Johnson, Secretary of State Dean Rusk, and Secretary of Defense Robert McNamara to justify the horror. About the same time, television brought images of sheriff's deputies in Selma, Alabama, clubbing black men simply trying to walk across a bridge. It brought graphic pictures of police dogs and fire hoses ripping through young black marchers in Birmingham. After a commercial break, we saw angry mobs beating up draft card burners in Boston.

And then it began to dawn on me, and I acknowledged it with a heavy heart, that Vietnam was no aberration, Vietnam was a mirror of U.S. attitudes and actions. I marched with King against the war in 1968.

Church structures, I felt, were moving with glacial slowness to embrace the direction of Vatican II, especially as it applied to the war in Vietnam. My impatience led me into conflict with many of my brother Dominicans and with the mainstream of U.S. society. My sense of isolation, except from those I came to identify with as comrades in the peace movement, led to a desire for intimacy and affirmation I was not experiencing as a priest.

Discovery

At a time when so many social and ecclesiastical structures were being called into question, I applied for laicization, was granted it fairly quickly, and married at the end of 1969. I was fortunate to marry a kindred spirit, Janice Searles, who had peace ideals, wanted to make the world better, and had spent a long time in the religious life herself, as Sister Janice Marie, S.P.

Although I had been intensely involved in the movement to stop the war in Vietnam since 1965, I didn't look at it particularly as a nonviolent activity. In reality, some of it wasn't. I just knew, on the basis of my study and experience, that the war should end. Shortly after we married, Janice was completing her graduate studies at Mundelein College in Chicago. She chose to do her master's thesis on nonviolence, seeing it as an overarching idea for the social concerns we both shared. Her research got me as interested in Gandhi's theories as I was already interested in King's tactics. The writings of Gandhi began to open up a whole new horizon. The nonviolence of Gandhi and King gave me a new peace vision of what the world could become. I, too, came to see the value of nonviolence as a life-affirming and life-changing force. I re-read Pope John XXIII's encyclical *Pacem in Terris*. I began to appreciate that the courageous, persevering posture of active nonviolence might well be the most appropriate personal attitude toward the deeply distressing diseases of racism and war. Like many others before me, I came to see the value of nonviolence as a life-affirming and life-changing force.

New Church Structures

In the summer of 1970 we moved to Memphis. I had been offered a teaching position and Janice, with her new master's degree in religious studies, was asked to organize an adult education program for Catholics. Several months after we arrived, the new Diocese of Memphis was created, carving the western third of the state away from the Diocese of Nashville. Janice right away met the first bishop, a courtly monsignor from Virginia named Carroll Dozier.

As we got to know him better we learned he had had a special interest in peace since his Rome years as a theology student in Mussolini-dominated Italy. Now, in Memphis, he wanted to make peace the theme of his first pastoral letter to the people of the new diocese. Janice and I were invited to be part of an advisory group to craft the document.

We first gathered around Bishop Dozier's dining room table to begin work in the fall of 1971. His opening remark was that his pastoral letter would follow Thomas Aquinas, who had laid out conditions under which war could be justified, the foundation of what had become known as the Just War Theory. In the months of dialogue that followed around that dining room table, new ideas emerged. During those working sessions, in the open discussions he encouraged, his thinking had evolved in the direction of nonviolence. When his pastoral letter was ready for publication, Bishop

Dozier wrote that "war was no longer tolerable for a Christian." He would later say publicly, "The Just War Theory should be locked away in the same drawer as the Flat Earth Theory."

Bishop Dozier's peace letter brought him to the attention of a group of Catholics on the east coast who were planning to start a U.S. section of Pax Christi, the international Catholic peace movement. He, along with Bishop Thomas Gumbleton of Detroit, was asked to provide episcopal leadership. Bishop Dozier asked Janice and me to accompany him in that early effort. Because of him we became involved in Pax Christi USA in its first years and were pleased to join with veteran peace people like Eileen Egan and Gordon Zahn in helping Pax Christi spread.

Our journey to a spirituality of nonviolence had taken some unexpected turns.

Chapter 2

Personal Spirituality

Spirituality is often defined as our relationship with God. Put another way, spirituality is aligning our innermost being with the Way of the Cosmos. Spirituality is more than devotion to career and family, deeper than concern about health and welfare, beyond merely dealing with life as it happens. Spirituality is our effort to get our total being right, ultimately right, or at least as right as we can given everything we know.

It is our "attitude," in the sense of the attitude of a space capsule in the proper position for reentry. Spirituality is a lifelong effort, an ongoing discernment of the most significant realities and Reality. At times it may result in a realignment. When we get a new fix on the Way of the Cosmos, or when we find ourselves in a new way of life, we adjust our spirituality accordingly.

These are anxious times—of wars and rumors of wars, of fear and suspicion, of material superabundance for a few and plaguing poverty for most. We live in a violent and dangerous world. Muggings, drug abuse, hijackings, suicide bombings, many forms of discrimination, corporate theft, terrorism, and pre-emptive wars are perennial possibilities. There is mistrust of governments, lies by the powerful and uncertainty in the many.

Most people, in the midst of the murk, desire something better, something more meaningful. Witness the appeal that televangelists and mega-churches have for many, the appeal that charismatic music groups have for others. They strike a chord, point to something arousing, something at the same time comforting, beyond daily dreariness.

Almost everyone has a need to feel part of something greater than the self. Traditional churches, synagogues, and mosques still satisfy that hunger for some. National, cultural, or economic ideologies do it for others. But, for many, religious institutions and prevailing ideologies have become so much a part of the status quo, the predictable humdrum of existence, that they no longer satisfy as fully as they once did.

We may choose to withdraw from all this as much as we can and pursue a spirituality of private prayer and personal communion with the Absolute. But if instead of withdrawal we choose engagement, we need a spirituality that works for us, a practical spirituality that will guide us along the way and inspire us to contribute constructively and persevere faithfully.

Peacemakers' Spirituality

For those deeply concerned about true peace with justice in our personal, political, and global lives, a spirituality based on active nonviolence is highly appropriate to our tumultuous times. And for those concerned that our lives be deeply influenced by Jesus of Nazareth, a spirituality based on nonviolence is in harmony with his actions and teachings, especially when we look at the Gospels through what Richard McSorley called "peace eyes." The more we understand Jesus, the more we appreciate him as the Nonviolent Christ, our guide and inspiration.

A spirituality based on active nonviolence has immediate practical consequences. It provides a comprehensive philosophy of life, giving us an overview, an interpretation of events, of history, of nature, an insight into what's really happening around us. It guides us in getting along with others, neither giving in nor imposing our will but seeking what is of truth and goodness in all. It is also practical in helping improve the self and giving a deeper and healthier understanding of the world as it is and as it can become. It puts us in spiritual communion with those millions of sisters and brothers around the world who are attempting to deal constructively and creatively with what seems like ever-more pervasive violence.

It Works

It is not only in the context of spiritual need that I find the theory and practice of active nonviolence so appealing, but also in the pragmatic context of getting results. The nonviolence pioneered by Gandhi in India and King in the United States has been used successfully in labor union strikes, calling attention to wars, farmworker boycotts, civil rights and liberation movements of all kinds—grand actions for political freedom and social change. Besides a tactic for social improvement and a guide to our everyday encounters with other people, it can also help us cope with stress, that lurking giant of whose malevolent presence we are increasingly aware and respectful. Just as active nonviolence has from time to time and place to place transformed the social scene, it can transform our personal lives.

King had shown how nonviolence could change the racial scene, could begin to overcome centuries of abuse and discrimination by white people, and help African Americans and white Americans look on each other and themselves with a heightened sense of shared humanity. His tragic death by an assassin's bullet robbed us of his developing ideas about how nonviolence could regulate dealings with other people, and what he meant by being nonviolent with himself.

Every time we're faced with a conflict in our personal lives, any kind of conflict, we have an opportunity to practice nonviolence. Active nonviolence can extend deep into our lives and bring about an inward personal transformation analogous to social transformations such as those in the United States in the 1950s and 1960s and India in the 1920s, 1930s, and 1940s. In his book *War Is a Force that Gives Us Meaning*, reporter Chris Hedges was referring to the majority of people in the world to whom war gives a terrible but deep meaning. But active nonviolence gives a significantly different and much better meaning for a growing minority. Its meaning is in becoming more fully human, more spiritually alive, as we consciously let the philosophy of nonviolence permeate our dealings with others and with ourselves.

Chapter 3

Foundations

One of the key words Gandhi used in expressing the meaning of nonviolence was *ahimsa,* literally "non-harm," the refusal to hurt others. It's the rock bottom of nonviolence. A second key word was *satyagraha* (a combination of the words for "truth" and "holding firmly"), sometimes called "truth force," holding on to what is true and good, striving to bring about more humane conditions for people and society. King called it "soul force."

Concentrating only on the non-harm aspect of nonviolence has led many to think of it as something negative. The most common misunderstanding about nonviolence is that it is a non-doing, a passivity, a refusal to be violent. Many times people who want to avoid trouble, who sidestep confrontation, are said to be nonviolent. They may simply be evasive.

Gandhi's *satyagraha,* holding firmly to truth, leads to disciplined action. The Sanskrit word *sat,* truth, at root means "is" or "being." It implies that the most fundamental truth is existence itself. Gandhi gave a humanitarian twist to it by insisting that truth is whatever is life-affirming, whatever contributes to a fuller human existence.

Gandhi's criterion for whether an action is true or false, good or bad, was whether or not it is conducive to human well-being. His particularized meaning of truth is in harmony with Vatican II's stress on "the duty to build a better world," what it called "the birth of a new humanism." When we engage in this demanding work, we are pointed in the direction of truth as Gandhi understood it.

The nonviolence of Gandhi and King begins with the recognition that we're talking about something positive, about action, about doing. The nonviolence of Gandhi and King is anything but negative, and it is certainly not evasive. It does include the element of refusing to hurt others. But it is much more; it is vigorous, positive, and assertive *activity*. A nonviolent person does things— speaks, walks, gesticulates, intervenes—and is constantly active in mind and heart, trying to figure out what is happening and looking for effective ways of persuasion.

Gandhi rightly insisted that we cannot always know for certain what is true in the sense of conducive to human well-being, what in fact is contributing to building a better world. None of us has a monopoly on truth. He saw this as another reason for *ahimsa*. We don't have the right to hurt someone for violating truth because we may be seeing only a partial aspect of it. They may have another aspect.

In nonviolence we try to create an atmosphere to clarify the truth. So we need to know whatever there is of truth in another's position as well as our own, whether the other at the moment is our spouse, a child at home, a colleague, a supervisor at work, an intrusive salesperson, a police officer writing a ticket, our city council representative, or the President of the United States. We listen, we learn, then we act. And we continue to listen and learn, so that we will act more effectively.

Realistic Requirements

Nonviolence does not insist on perfection. In our search for truth we're going to cause some harm. Although Gandhi taught that we should strive for *ahimsa*, he recognized that we are all caught up in some degree of *himsa*. He was convinced that a person cannot go through a single day without inflicting pain. Whether we intend it or not, we will hurt others in some way.

But what we can do is to become increasingly sensitive to the damage we inflict, the emotional hurt, the unintended slight, and try to lower its level or reverse its direction. We won't eliminate it altogether, but we will cut it back as our awareness becomes more acute.

Nonviolent action takes courage. Gandhi was so insistent on this that he said if ever it came to a choice between violence or cowardice, we should choose violence. It is easy to sit back and let unpleasant things happen when we don't have the heart to try to correct them. But such a *laissez-faire* attitude is a counterfeit nonviolence. King called it "stagnant passivity." True nonviolence takes inner energy, desire, and a willingness to risk.

Nonviolent action may be only a touch, a look, a calm word, but it always reaches out to help. The best definition I know of genuine nonviolence is *positive action for true human good, using only means that help and do not harm.*

It is not haphazard, a restless expenditure of energy, but action toward a greater good. We might call it courteous assertion. Courtesy, respect for others, is a consequence of the principle of non-harm. The assertion, moving ahead courageously for truth, justice, humaneness, is based on *satyagraha*, the search for truth.

Foundations of Goodness and Forgiveness
Active nonviolence is based on a definite set of beliefs. The first is about individual people—that they are basically good. This is the underlying meaning of the affirmation that life is sacred, that everyone is a daughter or son of God. Some Eastern religions express it as the God within, or the universality of the Buddha nature. Everyone has the potential to reach spiritual heights, to obtain enlightenment, to be saved. No matter how deplorably they act at times, people, we believe, are fundamentally worthy of respect.

"Violence" comes from the Latin *violare*, which means to injure or dishonor. In nonviolence we refuse to injure or dishonor another, physically or otherwise, because everyone is valuable. Even when we're attacked or treated unjustly, we acknowledge the radical goodness in our opponents.

And we forgive them. But forgive the way King described forgiveness: not a sentimental blurring of a past offense, pretending it didn't happen, but a conscious refusal not to let past offenses block the building of a present relationship. Forgive, but don't forget. Keep your eyes open. The same set of circumstances can produce the same results, the same offense or conflict, again. We want to see it coming the next time, and ward it off. But forgive now, let the affront pass, and be ready to start over again, because everyone can do better.

In this positive way, which is not sentimental or wimpy, we can appreciate Jesus' advice to forgive—again and again. How often, as many as seven times? "I do not say to you seven times, but seventy times seven" (Matthew 18:22). He wasn't being literal, meaning to forgive 490 times and that's enough. His arithmetic was symbolic, combining the number for perfection, seven, with the number for multitude, ten. Seven squared times ten is another way of putting seventy times seven. Jesus meant forgive again and again, times without number.

Gandhi said, "Forgiveness is the ornament of the brave." Forgive, rather than lashing out to hurt. Forgive, rather than punish. Forgive, because everyone is still capable of decency even after doing something wrong. Jesus taught that the way we forgive others is the measure of being forgiven ourselves. "Forgive us our debts as we forgive our debtors" (Matthew 6:12).

We know that we ourselves have a dark side. We can hurt others by a quick retort, one-upping, putting someone down in order to feel superior, maneuvering our way into a favorable position at someone else's expense. We acknowledge this in ourselves at the same time we recognize it in others. But the most effective way of responding to it is not in kind, not continuing the cycle, but instead, with patient engagement, reaching out to help rather than to hurt. As the Pax Christi USA saying has it, "Violence ends where love begins."

When we're attacked or treated unjustly, our foundational faith leads us to acknowledge the radical goodness in our opponents and refrain from striking back, from hurting in return. Most of the time when we treat people as basically good, they respond positively. Sometimes they don't. But our conviction, as practitioners of active nonviolence, is that when they do mistreat us we have a better way of handling it than to be violent in return.

And it works on a smaller scale, closer to home. Shortly after I read King's ideas on forgiveness, my wife Janice and I had a disagreement. Whatever it was about, we quickly turned it to some past pattern of behavior—"You always act that way." Then something clicked, an inspiration or a grace. I remember thinking, let's not get diverted to the past this time; let's stay on the present issue. Somehow we were able to put the past aside and concentrate on what we were arguing about. We discussed our difference, whatever it was, and were able to resolve it rather quickly. It was such a relief not to get bogged down in past behavior, not to nurse hurt feelings. Nonviolence on a personal scale became instantly practical for me!

Cooperation over Competition

A second major belief on which nonviolence is based concerns the preferred way of human interaction: the best form is cooperation, working together in a spirit of sharing. We need others if we want to be whole ourselves. The human race has survived because of cooperation, not competition. Gandhi thought cooperation so important that he called it "a law of our species."

This belief is reinforced pragmatically every time we see that cooperation improves the quality of our life. When we contribute something to others, it enhances our own feeling of well-being. And, when we relax and let others into our life, we benefit tangibly by the added richness they bring.

Jesus said, "You know that those who are recognized as rulers over the Gentiles lord it over them, and their great ones make their authority over them felt. But it shall not be so among you. Rather, whoever wishes to be great among you will be your servant" (Mark 10:42b-43). True power comes from working with others, not over them or against them; truth sought together brings people power.

Gandhi taught the same approach. His goal was not just the liberation of India from the British, but a transformation of Indian society. He believed strongly that the attitude of all toward all should be that of service. He said that a person devoted "to service with a clear conscience will day by day grasp the necessity for it in greater measure, and will continually grow richer in faith."

Cosmic Good

The third belief that undergirds active nonviolence is that not only individual people, but the universe itself is, on balance, good. Despite tornadoes, floods, forest fires, volcanoes, wild animals, poisonous plants, earthquakes, and a tenuous ozone layer, we believe that the whole thing tilts—ever so slightly, perhaps— toward good. The seven-day creation story ends with "And God saw everything that God had made, and behold, it was very good" (Genesis 1:31a). The Psalmist sang, "The heavens declare the glories of God" (Psalms 19:1a).

Our intuition is that what we call the cosmos—the randomness, the vastness, and the complexity of the physical universe, along with its intangible dimensions—works in some as yet unfathomed way for wholeness. We believe the whole is more conducive to growth than to suffering. King referred to it: "The arc of the moral universe is long, but it bends toward justice." When we nonviolently pursue that justice, that humaneness, Vatican II's "better world," whether in the streets or right at home, we have what King called "cosmic companionship."

Liberating Discipleship

Nonviolence is a way of looking at the world and at the people around us and saying *no* to the distress and ugliness, the exploitation and violence, but also saying *yes* to all which can heal the distress, transform the ugliness, and remove the exploitation. That doesn't just mean *saying* no to the violence, but *doing* something to end it. Seek the truth by acting for the truth.

Our active grappling with conflict may well lead us to a point where we can get hurt, emotionally often, but physically sometimes. We face criticism, and may face worse, for the stances we take. At those critical times the spirit of nonviolence leads us to accept suffering rather than inflict it. To Christians it's called the theology of the cross. "If you wish to come after me, you must deny your very self, take up your cross, and follow in my footsteps. If you would save your life, you'll lose it, but if you lose your life for my sake, you'll save it" (Mark 8:34a-35). We have to be prepared to accept the hurt ourselves, rather than impose it on others. Gandhi put it dramatically: "Rivers of blood may have to flow before we gain our freedom, but it must be our blood...Suffering is infinitely more powerful than the law of the jungle for converting the opponent and opening...ears which are otherwise shut to the voice of reason."[1] When I think of rivers of blood, any public or private criticism—even arrest and imprisonment—I may face is paltry by comparison. We free ourselves from the manipulative attempts of others to the extent that we are willing to suffer, maybe a little, but sometimes more.

The truth of nonviolence goes against the conventional micro-wisdom of narrow self-interest. A life based on maximizing one's personal fulfillment, pleasure, or joy lacks real satisfaction. Nonviolence transmutes the pursuit of happiness from self-serving to self-giving. It involves openness, responsiveness, and a certain flowing with events rather than always trying to put one's stamp on them. Gandhi called nonviolence an "experiment in truth." When we decide to make our lives as nonviolent as possible, we too will engage in much experimentation. At such times we may be criticized for our inconsistency, or be told that we're misguided. But we don't back down.

Jesus did say to his followers, "Your light must shine before others" (Matthew 5:16a). It should shine not for personal adulation, but for the benefit of the others. And, paradoxically, it's good for us in turn. Martin Luther King knew that those who set out on the road to nonviolence would become better than they were. He wrote, "Another of the major strengths of the nonviolent weapon is its strange power to transform and transmute the individuals who subordinate themselves to its disciplines, investing them with a cause that is larger than themselves. They become, for the first time, *somebody*, and they have, for the first time, the courage to be free."[2]

Nonviolence is in harmony with the deeper truth, the paradox that in giving we receive, in loving we are loved, in dying we rise to a new life.

Part Two

Nonviolence Toward Myself

Humility, Thomas Aquinas said, is acknowledging the truth about ourselves. Virtually everyone who reads this book would consider himself or herself a "good person." No plaudits, no crowns, no headlines, no back-patting. But "good" in the sense of trying to be decent, honest, hard-working, more or less successful in making it through life. "Good people" are aware of shortcomings. "Good people" get upset by job frustrations, cut corners here and there, may not always be responsive to someone who needs help. We all have a shadow side. And we all have gifts—abilities and talents that are uniquely ours. Guided by the nonviolent Christ we can acknowledge what is best and honestly face what is less desirable. We can also discern forces in our surroundings which harass us, press in, or are upsetting and look for ways to deal with them constructively. We can take principles and ideas about spirituality and nonviolence and apply them to ourselves.

Chapter 4

The Shadow

A popular radio drama of the 1940s began each episode with a low, mysterious voice intoning, "Who knows what evil lurks in the hearts of men?" After a slight pause came the answer: "The Shadow knows," followed by a disquieting laugh. This radio Shadow was an anonymous, secretive character who understood the criminal mind. Always on the side of law and order, he foiled a different plot every week.

As we seek to become nonviolent toward ourselves, it helps to look at a different Shadow, this one courtesy of psychoanalyst Carl Jung. Jung gave the term to the dark, unpleasant side of the human psyche. This Shadow consists of traits and tendencies we don't like in ourselves, like greed or lust or laziness or self-righteousness. Lurking in our Shadows are those personal shortcomings we might uneasily perceive but want to shove out of sight because we're ashamed of them. Like the radio Shadow who knew the dark secrets of the criminal mind, our own personal Shadows contain many of the dark secrets of our own minds.

Most would prefer not to come to grips with these hidden shortcomings. Uncomfortable feelings percolate when we admit we have troublesome traits. We assume family and friends will disapprove if they know about them. So we're inclined to push this unsavory cluster down and away, removed from our conscious self-image.

But denying doesn't make them go away. Repressing can even intensify their presence, turning them into a cauldron of witches' brew simmering under the thin veneer of civilized behavior. And this witches' brew can be crippling, as Thomas Merton observed: "As long as we believe that we hate no one, that we are merciful, that we are kind by our very nature, we deceive ourselves, our hatred is merely smoldering under the gray ashes of complacent optimism. We are apparently at peace with everyone because we think we are worthy. That is to say we have lost the capacity to face the question of unworthiness at all."[1]

Showing Up

Precisely when we haven't come to grips with it, the Shadow's bottled-up energy shows up in abrupt behaviors that leave us wondering, "Why did I do that!" Sudden anger at a child's innocent antics or an inappropriate denouncement of a colleague's mistake may leave us surprised. "I guess I just lost control." "I don't know what got into me." Or "the devil made me do it." Because our conscious mind has not acknowledged these hidden traits, they are apt to express themselves in disguised or distorted ways, in impulsive actions we don't fully understand.

When I don't acknowledge them in myself, they exert pressure, make me uneasy. One of the most common psychological mechanisms from our Shadow is projecting an unpleasant characteristic onto others and then disliking them because of it. I can alleviate my anxiety by perceiving these flaws in others and looking down on them for it. If I am greedy, I can keep an eagle eye out for avarice. If deep down I want to be in control, I resent efforts to control me. If I'm ashamed of my sexuality, I can point to adulterers or prostitutes and feel clean when I consider them sinners.

When our Shadows prompt those of us who are financially secure to dislike people who are economically poor, it's easy to lapse into the familiar syndrome of blaming the victim. "They're poor because they're lazy. It's their own fault. They should get out and get a job and work for a living." We feel relieved of whatever responsibility we might have for their situation—our complicity, perhaps, in the shutdown of jobs in the area when a business moves to Mexico or to China. Or our support of an attack on a distant country instead of a campaign for decent housing at home. Or white flight and the destruction of an area's infrastructure.

Fear of Death

One of the most common ingredients in one's Shadow is a sense of inadequacy, of vulnerability. On one level everyone experiences some degree of insecurity. But on a deeper level a sense of vulnerability stems from the temporariness of our existence. We know we're going to die. At some time in the future, distant or near, our familiar existence will cease. Life as we know it will stop, finally and definitely.

The threat of termination can be terrifying. It's much easier to refuse to think about it. Death is shoved into the depths of the Shadow. It is probably the strongest of the Furies that harass us, and the one most of us are most anxious to ignore into oblivion. A common way of compensating for the terror of termination is to seek to control as much of our immediate surroundings as we can. We seek it, and we often get it. But it doesn't provide the relief it promised. It's easy to be drawn further into the illusion that power over others is a way to compensate for feelings of vulnerability. And so we have lynchings, and pogroms, and pre-emptive wars.

Accepting the inevitability of our own death is difficult, but necessary for personal wholeness. Francis of Assisi called it "Sister Death," and felt at peace. Traditional Christian spirituality encouraged meditation on death. We all have to go sometime. Acknowledging this insistent fact of life goes a long way toward coming to grips with one's Shadow, harnessing its energy and turning it to positive good for ourselves and for those with whom we live and move and have our being.

Shadow Boxing

It's better by far to recognize one's Shadow and deal with it constructively, grapple with it nonviolently. Jung suggested that this constellation of characteristics shows up in dreams as feelings we wouldn't appreciate in daily living. Reflecting on these dream images, he believed, can yield significant clues.

We can also get a good glimpse of our Shadows by looking at people we don't like, and focusing on what it is that irritates us. More than likely, we'll find those very traits deep in our own makeup, covered over, masked from view. When we don't face them in ourselves, we're likely to be upset with them in others. The self-righteous "America First" proponent, constantly denouncing the aggression of enemy nations, is projecting. The guardian of public morals who searches out and examines obscene material to protect others from it is probably projecting. This doesn't mean that others' offensive behavior is purely imaginary, but it does mean the projector's response is dictated more by inner emotional imbalance than by the perceived irregularities.

What we're after is getting to know our Shadows, bringing them out into the light of our consciousness. When we take the plunge and stir around in the darkness of our psyche to see what's really there, when we look our Shadows in the eye and make friends, we become more whole, more integral persons.

Chapter 5

Our Gifts

We are born male or female. We have inherited genetic traits of height, shape, and color, plus physical and mental ability. All of us have a unique texture to our personalities. We are of a certain age and getting older.

All of our gifts have definite advantages, and some limitations. We have the ability to enhance our gifts, as well as to debase them. We have a certain amount of control over our own lives. Nonviolence toward ourselves includes taking positive steps to nurture what we have been given and to be grateful for what we have achieved. And we don't have to fret if we can't do everything well. As Eileen Egan once said, "No one has all the gifts."

Jesus was clear about the importance of healthy self-love. It's the foundation of our respect and love for others. "You shall love your neighbor as yourself" (Matthew 22:39b).

Taking care of our gifts includes responsibility for our physical condition. It does not mean pampering or primping, but rather seeing that what we eat and drink is generally healthful, that we exercise sufficiently so that our body functions properly. We keep ourselves in adequate physical shape, not (too much) overweight, fairly strong, moderately agile.

Gandhi insisted that *satyagrahis* take care of their appearance. He was always meticulous about his own personal cleanliness and demanded that those in the movement be clean and neat, too. He compared it to a soldier, who is required to have every button in place, uniform pressed, boots polished—not because the soldier will be clean and neat in battle, but to foster the soldier's own self-respect, and to make a good appearance to others. For Gandhi, cleanliness was not a stuffy, middle-class, "respectable" virtue, but an elemental expression of nonviolence. Good appearance is a way of saying that we care enough to make our immediate environment favorable for ourselves and others.

We keep our mind alert and spirit lively through reading, meditating, sharing with friends, listening to people who know more than we do. We accept the fact that some people are smarter, and that I am what I am with the talents that have been given to me. I don't have to be among the best and the brightest, but I should use fully the intelligence which I have been granted.

Then there is our personality profile. Some of us are extroverts; some are introverts. Some are feelers; others are thinkers. Some are very intuitive; others are less so. Some are spontaneous; others prefer to be more organized. None of these is necessarily better or worse. All of us can smooth out our rough edges. Introverts can learn the art of conversation; feelers can take time to digest ideas. Spontaneous souls can slow down occasionally, and meticulous organizers can loosen up. It's what we do with our attributes and with our limitations that matters, loving ourselves properly so that we can love our neighbors fully.

Nonviolence toward self includes accepting one's time in life. I think of ages twenty to forty as the Learning Years, forty to sixty as the Command Years, and from sixty on as the Wisdom Years. Youth has its attractive features—energy, physical agility, resilience. Middle age has other benefits, like the experience that comes from having been places and done things. The latter years, too, have their own unique assets: a career completed, a family nurtured, friends appreciated, a degree of serenity from having navigated life's bumps and potholes. It helps to accept wherever we are on the spectrum, not yearning for the forever-elusive fountain of youth. As Shelley Douglass has said, "claim your age." It's one of our gifts.

Half Full or Half Empty

A sign of progress toward inner peace is when we're able to look at what's troubling us not so much as obstacles that oppress, but as challenges to face. A pessimist concentrates on the bad things that could happen. An optimist thinks about ways to deal with the challenges. The sight of an elderly person with a serene smile despite aches and pains can make my day.

Those who confront a predicament believing the outcome will be favorable are more likely to achieve the favorable outcome than if they believe the opposite. Dr. Bernie Siegel, a New York cancer specialist, said that when he tells patients they have cancer, he gets one of two reactions. Some respond in despair, "When am I going to die?" Others react with, "What can I do to fight it?" The latter, he found, have a remarkable rate of recovery. The others usually die in a relatively short time.

As we concentrate on life-affirming ways of dealing with our Shadows, taking prudent care of ourselves, affirming our good qualities, accepting where we are, we are becoming more nonviolent toward ourselves. Most of us aren't going to be celebrities or superstars. Our lot will be to get up in the morning and face whatever the day brings, stumbling over one or another unforeseen obstacle, trying to meet our responsibilities. We do some things nicely, others haphazardly. We make mistakes. We try to get by. We may not achieve artistic brilliance or world fame, we may not do heroic deeds or move mountains, but the way we meet the multiple challenges that confront us every day makes a difference—in our own lives and in the lives of those around us.

Chapter 6

Stress and Worry

At the height of the sanitation workers' strike that brought Martin Luther King Jr. to Memphis in 1968, two young black leaders of a group known as the Invaders arranged to meet with him. King's aides were uneasy. The Invaders were tough, bristling for an argument; they wanted drastic action.

As soon as King appeared the atmosphere changed. "When he came in the room, it seemed like all of a sudden there was a real rush of wind and everything just went out and peace and calm settled over everything," one of the Invaders said. "You could feel peace around that man. I have never seen anyone that looked like peace, and that man looked like peace. I was kind of shocked."

What King did when he met those young men is the effect I'd like to have on others. When I'm relatively peaceful within myself I can at least partially achieve it. But when I'm anxious, I communicate my nervousness and people get edgy. As Mary Lou Kownacki put it, "Everyone starts rearranging the furniture." When we're calm, it helps others to be calm.

In the process of making our hearts more nonviolent, it helps to look at those elements in our personal and social environment that are upsetting, that make us irritable. Life usually doesn't practice *ahimsa* toward us. Stress can be a nagging worry that discolors our lives, robs us of inner peace, and infects us with higher anxiety. Everyone is susceptible to unavoidable accidents or natural disasters or human perversity—from tornadoes to terrorists, from crashes to cancer. We're better able to handle these mega-matters if we have learned to deal with the daily pressures that push on us much of the time.

Don't Do It

Sometimes, in the spirit of *ahimsa* toward ourselves, we have to refuse to take on yet one more project, go to one more meeting, answer one more phone call. At times we have to say no. The trouble is that people involved in a nonviolent approach to life have a strong concern for others. Yet resources are limited; results are imperfect. More needs to be done. Always more. And it's all worth doing. It's all deserving work. Yes, this meeting is important. Yes, this caller needs attention. Yes, this lonely or sick person needs help. But to be nonviolent toward ourselves we sometimes have to say no.

The problem in working toward nonviolence is not that we need encouragement to *do*, but rather we sometimes need encouragement *not to do*. That's hard. It makes us feel guilty.

But Jesus sometimes did it, sometimes had to say no. He recognized the need to take a break, to get away. After feeding the five thousand, "he went up on a mountainside by himself to pray" (Matthew 14:23a). It was hard to get away. People wouldn't leave him alone. "Jesus left that place and went to the vicinity of Tyre. He entered a house and did not want anyone to know it; yet he could not keep his presence secret" (Mark 7:24). So he sometimes had to slip away furtively, to find the solitude he needed. "Very early in the morning, while it was still dark, Jesus got up, left the house, and went off to a solitary place, where he prayed" (Mark 1:35). He knew he needed the quiet time.

High-Tech Pressures

Anyone's job can be a source of stress. Just holding on to it, in times of un- and underemployment, downsizing and outsourcing, is anxiety-producing. We want our performance to be up to par. Even the most rewarding position involves concentration on details, much plodding, and dull minutiae. I find solace in the wisdom of a veteran colleague who once observed, "There's not a job in the world that's not ninety percent janitoring." Or as Thomas Edison put it, "Genius is one percent inspiration and ninety-nine percent perspiration." When the work presses in, I grit my teeth and get on with the janitoring, exert the perspiration. Plunge in to get the job done. If the downsizing or outsourcing happens and I'm one of its victims, I'll be better able to face it if I have the calm that comes from my efforts at being nonviolent toward myself. Technology has brought us cell phones, satellite communications, myriad television channels, and the genie called a computer. At the other end of the telephone's ring might be a friendly voice or some good news. But often it turns out to be unwanted solicitations, favors requested, announcements of yet another meeting— more demands on time and energy. The computer with its daily load of e-mails sits in accusatory silence until we yield to its demand to call up today's bundle, read everything, answer many, get on with it before we can get away from it.

But a telephone does not always have to be picked up when it rings; the computer does not always have to be turned on. Answering machines can store important calls; e-mails can accumulate in cyberspace. Because incessant outside communications impose stress, we can handle them on our own terms, not the machines'.

Although they didn't have telephones and computers in Jesus' day, he recognized this kind of stress and tried to deal with it. Jesus knew that he and his apostles needed some relief. "Let's go," he said, "to a quiet place and get some rest" because "people were coming and going in great numbers, and they had no opportunity even to eat" (Mark 6:31). Those people probably had genuine needs, but Jesus tried to avoid being drained all the time. He had to take a break.

Another time, after a particularly intense day of healing, "when Jesus saw a crowd around him, he gave orders to cross to the other side of the lake" (Matthew 8:18). He had had enough. Despite the furious storm that came up he was so tired that he fell asleep in the boat (Matthew 8:24).

Always Enough Time

Most of us know people who spend long hours on the job, then when they're at home are always fixing something around the house or building something in the basement. Or they're out shopping. They seem addicted to activity. They speak with pride about "keeping busy," about "not having enough time" to do all that they have to do.

Because the slippery self never seems to be in quite the condition we want it, we can also succumb to the seduction of an endless preoccupation with self-improvement. It's possible to become so obsessed with one's imperfections, so desirous of shaping up this or that aspect of our personality or appearance that we find little time for anything else. The way I look at it is: keep the infrastructure in place and in reasonably good repair. Check it now and then, but don't spend too much time on it.

Busyness is one of the characteristics of our age. It's easy to get caught up in the swirl of activity, much of which is worthwhile. Some isn't though. If we would become more nonviolent toward ourselves, we need to take a hard look at the temptation to busyness. Urgent matters demand immediate attention, like an accident that needs rushing to the emergency room, or a flood in the bathroom, or a sick child. At the opposite end are the nitty-gritty realities that make up so much of our day, what philosopher Jean-Paul Sartre called the "facticity" of life. In our home we say, "The chores need to be done."

Between the chores and the emergencies we fit in our peace work—dealing with labor exploitation, campaigning to prevent a war. Elise Boulding said, "Our time is too short to do anything but what is conducive to peace."

Typical time management theory details ways of becoming more efficient by getting more done in a shorter period. It works well, if we adopt it wisely. If we don't, the result is that we find we have more to do. As Cyril Northcote Parkinson observed, work tends to expand to fill the time allotted for it. If we can tame the temptation to busyness, we find that we always have enough time. What we do with it expresses our beliefs about the meaning of our life.

Creative Worry

Well-meaning people often say, "Oh, don't worry about that," as though worry can be turned off like a faucet. They're concerned about our well-being; they would like us to stop being anxious. We may appreciate their concern, but it's hard to take their advice. Until we can come up with a solution to what's bothering us, we can't just stop worrying on the spot.

In fact, it may at times be irresponsible not to worry. It's true that some do it inordinately, but worry itself can be healthy. All of us at times have pressing problems about which we have to be concerned to avoid damage to ourselves or others.

But we have to worry creatively, not destructively. Creative worry may involve setting aside some time each day, a half hour or so, and spending it on *active worrying*. Imagine our mental radar scanning the day, the time ahead. When a threat blip shows up, something causing anxiety, concentrate on it, worry about it, maybe write it down. Journaling can help alleviate anxiety. Then let it go for a while. Sometimes, in the absence of concerted concentration, a solution will pop up later or a way to proceed will suddenly appear. If it doesn't, well, I've worried enough about it for a while.

Sometimes it helps to recall Jesus' advice, "Therefore do not worry about tomorrow, for tomorrow will worry about itself. Each day has enough trouble of its own" (Matthew 6:34). The exercise proposed by the Buddhist monk Thich Nhat Hanh can be helpful:

> Breathing in, I calm my body.
> Breathing out, I smile.
> Dwelling in the present moment
> I know this is a wonderful moment.[1]

Buddhists say that when we're walking we should know we're walking, when we're feeling the wind we should know we're feeling the wind, when we're looking at flowers we should know we're looking at flowers—not thinking and worrying about what's going to happen in five minutes or tomorrow. I've found relief in concentrating for a few minutes on the flow of clouds in the sky. I begin to feel refreshed, a little more peaceful.

Genuinely slow, deep breathing has a physiologically calming effect. Smiling relaxes my facial muscles and contributes to a lessening of my inner tension. And then let go for a moment. Live in the immediate present. It's all I've really got. Eleanor Roosevelt said, "Yesterday is history; tomorrow is mystery; today is a gift."

Part Three

Everyday Nonviolence

We can help our neighborhoods and the nation become less violent by becoming more nonviolent ourselves, because there's no such thing as a neighborhood or a nation apart from its people. Day-to-day living is where we have the greatest opportunity to be nonviolent. We can consciously be aware of principles of nonviolence in our speech, our relationships with family and friends, our career and professional life. Instead of the too common behaviors of aggression, competition, and winning through intimidation, there is a helpful, healing alternative in active, positive nonviolence. Through practice it can become almost a reflexive response in everyday life. In addition to being nonviolent toward ourselves, we need to be nonviolent toward others, through our speech, public relations (everyday interactions with the world), and leadership.

Chapter 7

A Nonviolent Dialect

In the Buddhist tradition a person on the road to spiritual improvement is encouraged early on to work on his or her language. On the Buddha's Eightfold Path to enlightenment, "right speech" is the third step, after "right views"—knowing in which direction to go—and "right aspirations"—deciding to go in that direction. Know what to do, and then decide to do it. Intellect and will. Then get practical.

The Buddha suggested the way to get practical is to start with our speech. It's an immediate area on which to concentrate, not only for anyone who might think the whole nonviolent package is too big to swallow at once, but also for those already familiar with nonviolence who haven't paid much attention to its possibilities in language. It's not all that difficult to become more aware of what we say and how we say it. But we have to concentrate on it.

Revealing Ourselves

In speaking we open ourselves to others, maybe a little, maybe a lot. When we speak, we talk about something perhaps as commonplace as the weather, or as complex as human relations. But in the act of speaking we also communicate something about ourselves. What comes out when we talk is a hint of our inner life, who we really are. Jesus said, "The things that come out of the mouth come from the heart" (Matthew 15:18a). We speak from what we are. It shows not only in the words we choose, but also our manner of speaking—calm or excited, peremptory or tentative.

This self-revelation occurs unless, of course, we're acting, pretending to be what we're not. Theatrical professionals undergo training to do this. Their job demands that they appear to mean their lines, no matter what they're feeling inside. We don't expect self-revelation from actors and actresses as they're performing. They know how to portray feelings they don't necessarily have, to say things that don't coincide with their inner self. That's hard to do consistently. To speak something different from what we are goes against our nature. That's why lie detectors work. Changes in body temperature and pulse rate are signs of the tension that accompanies saying something other than what we really feel. It's also why so many people in the entertainment business have problems with emotional soundness. Their profession calls for them constantly to be putting on a different face, pretending to be something they're not.

People in public life, too, often say things that are different from what they believe. But they don't always do it with the same skill. Much as we would like to trust them, we know they're primarily trying to persuade us to believe something or accept something. Political figures frequently say what they imagine their constituents want to hear rather than what they themselves really believe. Some are so poll-driven that, to stay in power, they tailor their words and demeanor according to the latest opinion surveys. And even when they are speaking authentically, we still can't be sure, because the very appearance of authenticity can also be an act. Insincerity may be a regrettable but inevitable accompaniment to public office. It may also be why many political figures resort to bizarre behavior in their off-camera lives, to compensate for the inner unrest caused by their public persona.

Jesus was getting at the dangerous effects of deliberately misspeaking when he warned that we would "have to give account on the day of judgment for every careless word" (Matthew 12:36). Something significant is at stake whenever we talk—the truth as we see it, and the truth about ourselves.

Ahimsa Talk

Nonviolent language will not be entirely new, but it's different enough to be called a dialect, a variation on common usage. First, it avoids hurting others directly, through shouting angrily, humiliating, lying. These are forms of violent speech. So is excessive obscene language, designed to shock. Although becoming more commonplace, so much so that we're in danger of developing an immunity to it, this kind of language may communicate an atmosphere of abuse.

A nonviolent dialect also excludes words or phrases whose original context is the world of damage and hurt, even though these are not intended. Sometimes people say, "fire away," when they're ready to be questioned. And if they don't answer the questions correctly, they get "blown away" or "shot down." Advertisers "target" a certain audience. An announcer gives "a blow by blow description." An editor "kills a story." These colorful expressions, often taken from military jargon, can be used rhetorically to good advantage. But they are drawn from actions that destroy property and hurt people.

As we become more aware of the connotations of what we're saying, we look for alternative expressions. Instead of saying, "fire away," we might ask, "What would you like to know?" Rather than "kill the story," we could simply say, "Don't print it." "They booby-trapped my project" can become "I ran into serious opposition." Eileen Egan suggested that for "kill two birds with one stone," we offer to "feed two birds with one crust."

A Practice of Prejudice

Conscious of *ahimsa*, we are increasingly sensitive to language that is sexist, racist, or ethnically disparaging. These usages have contributed to a tradition of discrimination that tolerated and often encouraged abuses against those considered weaker or secondary in society. A nonviolent dialect excludes racial slurs, anti-Semitic remarks, Polish—or any other ethnic—jokes.

When women were assumed to be inferior to men, it seemed natural to use masculine words referring to both genders. "A person should watch what he says." "We believe in brotherhood and fellowship." Anyone brought up when that grammar was taught as orthodox has to take care to adjust the syntax. "Policeman" or "fireman" may have been accurate when these professions were filled predominantly by males. Now we say "police officer" or "firefighter" or "spokesperson" or "chairperson." We don't classify occupation by gender, such as referring to a "male nurse" or a "lady doctor." "Fellowship" becomes "companionship" or "sharing." We also watch for language that excludes people.

A Matter of Manner

A nonviolent dialect involves not just what we say, but our tone of voice. Courtesy and consideration are its hallmarks. It's a matter of manner as well as a matter of words. Our voices are like musical instruments, embodying our emotions. Vocal tones can be gentle and soothing or sharp and demanding. Jumpy or excited speech has a place at jumpy or excited times. In normal conversations it can be jarring. If our sound is abrasive, no matter how well-intentioned, our words strike out stridently and cause sensitive people to draw back. But if our tone is smooth and supportive, others will feel more calm. (See chapter eighteen for more on the constructive role of anger.)

A simple request, "What time will you get home today?" can be spoken imperiously, pressing for an answer. "Where are you going?" with an emphasis on "going" and a downturn of voice communicates a demand. Asked in a soft way and ending in a slightly elevated tone, the same question will be heard as a desire for friendly sharing. The Irish lilt, words delivered lightly, with an upswing and a hint of smile, suggests gentleness rather than force, pleasure rather than pressure.

A nonviolent person, tuned in to the hearing needs of others, will be careful to speak loudly enough to be heard clearly, but not so loud as to be upsetting. A nonviolent dialect is spoken at a moderate level, neither shouting nor whispering. It also means being aware of different cultural patterns of speaking and the fact that humans are raised speaking many different languages. For instance, speaking speed is often a factor for people speaking or listening to a language that is not their first language. With a nonviolent dialect, we are careful not to speak too fast or indistinctly, being sensitive to the processing ability of the other.

Giving Advice—Less

I used to love to give advice, to interject my solution to some-one else's problem. Because, of course, I thought I knew what they should be doing or how they could improve. Someone would say, "I'm having a lot of trouble with my car." I might jump in, "I know this wonderful little shop that specializes in your make of car. You should take it there."

One psychologist calls advice like this "should-ies." When we provide a "should-ie," such as, "You should get more exercise," we put our personal force into the suggestion. The other person has to deal not just with my idea, but with my ego, not just with what I'm saying, but with what *I'm* saying. The pressure of my personality may make the person uncomfortable.

I couldn't understand why, when I started to give my solution to someone's problem, the other person would often stop talking, and then not follow my advice. It took me a long time to learn to go slow with suggestions. Now I believe it's usually better to sym-pathize than to advise. Now I would say, "That's too bad about your car." If I get a clear signal that someone is looking for sugges-tions, then I can offer a few, like telling about the little car repair shop, or the advantage of regular exercise. But I have to be sure they are genuinely looking. So often, what others really want to do is ventilate, not hear my advice. Deep down they know what needs to be done, or are confident they can figure it out for themselves.

Active Listening

One effective way of supporting a conversational partner is to respond directly to what has been said rather than interjecting one's own train of thought. Before I learned the importance of active listening, I frequently found myself interrupting. What the other person was saying would jog something in me, and I would blurt it out. A friend said, "Last week our house was broken into." I would interrupt, "We've had a lot of burglaries in our neighbor-hood, too." Someone I hadn't seen for a while said, "I had surgery on my knee." I would jump in, "I've just had a cataract removed." When I begin a train of thought and I'm interrupted by an enthusiastic conversation partner, I'm left hanging, awkward, a little frustrated. In the same way it must be abrasive to others when I interrupt, preventing the development of their thoughts. When I jump in like that I may be slighting the other, even being a bit rude. My enthusiasm might be attractive, but it may not compensate for the slight squelch I've just administered.

When I talk, I appreciate others showing they understand me, or at least have heard me. I can help others feel that way by affirming that I've heard what they've said, maybe by a question that encourages them to continue. "We went to Europe last summer." "Great. What countries did you visit?" An appropriate response could be only repeating their last words, encouraging further description. In what we say and how we say it, we try to avoid harm, and communicate in a helpful, supportive way.

Fine-Tuning the Heart

A good thing about a nonviolent dialect is that it is unilateral. We can initiate it ourselves. As with any language, it doesn't come automatically. It's a skill to be learned. A wife can help a husband, a friend help a friend. They can remind us, gently we hope, when we've gotten off the track, and give us occasional tips on verbal improvement.

Most of those with whom we converse won't be skilled in nonviolent speech. Some will be aggressive, asserting their own egos and putting others down. Some will talk much more than they listen. Others will tend to withdraw, cringe, and not take part in the conversation. Nonviolent speech means being quietly confident with the big talkers, sympathetic with the incessant talkers, gentle and nurturing with the fearful talkers.

What's in our heart comes out when we speak. But the causality goes both ways. When we deliberately use a nonviolent dialect, we fine-tune our heart as well. As we become more skilled in a nonviolent dialect, we will also be developing a more nonviolent heart.

Chapter 8

Public Relations

Martin Buber described two ways of being with others. One he called "I-Thou," a concerned sharing with those with whom we feel close, those we consider friends. The other was "I-It," where we keep people at a distance, treat them impersonally. In addition to these two, Harvey Cox suggested a third, which he called "I-You." It's for people whose paths cross ours in daily living but with whom we are not intimate—customers, checkout clerks, maintenance workers. These encounters comprise what I think of as our "public relations."

A nonviolent approach looks at everyone with whom we have these momentary meetings as a welcome "You" rather than an intimate "Thou" or an impersonal "It." We are pleasant, helpful when help is called for, but are not developing a close relationship. Showing respect and responsiveness makes everybody feel better, every human encounter a little richer. For some it might be simple courtesy and elementary politeness, a desire to make our human dealings more congenial. But it can also be a deliberate expression of personal nonviolence.

Body Language

As much as 70 percent (some say 90) of the information passing between people is communicated non-verbally. It pays to be aware of the way we comport ourselves. *Ahimsa* encourages us to make our nonverbal signals—gestures, posture, body movements—as positive and non-threatening as possible. Folding our arms can be taken as protective, indicating that we're holding ourselves in and putting up a barrier. Slouching may appear a sign of disrespect, even if we don't mean it that way and are only trying to be comfortable.

When meeting small children, I try to get down to their level or raise them up to mine. Making someone look up can be intimidating. When the two of us are on the same level physically the other becomes more responsive. I remember my first visit to a certain doctor's office. I was placed on a low sofa in front of his towering desk. "Now, what seems to be the problem?" I was not inspired to seek treatment from him.

Everyone has a sense of personal space, and this differs from culture to culture and also when people from different cultures or backgrounds are communicating. In the United States, many people tend to feel uncomfortable when someone comes within about two or three feet. It can create the need to back away a bit. So can solidly standing straight-ahead, face to face, which has been called the "challenge position." A more supportive way is facing at a slight turn. The subliminal message is that this offers an escape route, which fosters a more relaxed atmosphere. It is important to be aware of these differences: others may perceive how you are acting or even standing very differently from your intentions.

Eye contact, how much and what kind, is also important. Looking directly, especially when the other is talking, shows our interest in what is being said. If I don't give enough eye contact I appear evasive, or timid, or uninterested. But too much, more than five to seven seconds, can be intimidating. When someone continuously looks me in the eye, staring steadily, it makes me uncomfortable. Nonviolent eye contact is a relaxed and steady gaze, looking away occasionally, sensitive to what fosters a feeling of ease. Again, this differs from culture to culture and community to community, even within the same city, state, or country.

Driving

Other ordinary interactions offer chances to practice "I-you" public relations. One activity that is common for many of us is driving. In anxious times, road rage is characteristic. Even otherwise gentle people are tempted by their control of a powerful machine and the anonymity of traffic to vent their frustration.

Cutting in front, running the red, a sudden turn across traffic—all are signs of impatience with the flow of life.

But we can do something different. The way we handle ourselves behind the wheel is part of nonviolent public relations. Courteous assertion is the nonviolent way. We respect others and don't want to offend them, so we're courteous. If someone lets us in a line of cars, we wave thanks. And we let others in when we can do so without danger or annoying delay. At the same time we respect ourselves, so we're firm—gently, respectfully, but definitely. We drive crisply, straightforwardly, ready to yield out of courtesy, but taking the initiative when it doesn't offend.

Because of the need for prevention, we drive defensively. We delay a second or two before starting on a green light, in case someone is running the red. We are alert to other cars changing lanes without warning. Defensive driving is essential when so many are in a hurry, wrapped in their acclimatized cocoon with windows up and radios blasting, attention wandering because of their cell phone conversations.

We drive defensively, but we don't drive with defensiveness. When someone tries to cut in front of us, we don't hold our position without yielding to show them they can't do that. When another driver shouts at us because we made a mistake, we don't shout back to express our self-righteousness. The nonviolent driver has enough inner strength to absorb unpleasant antics without reacting with hostility. We don't want to take advantage of others, and we don't want them to take advantage of us. The way we drive, as with our other public relations, can be a genuine expression of active nonviolence.

Chapter 9

Nonviolent Leadership

It's been said that if you're leading and no one is following, you're only taking a walk. However, with nonviolent leadership, not only will we never walk alone, but people will work together in a humane cause.

Sometimes those in charge are designated or appointed whether or not they have the qualities of a good leader. A person committed to nonviolence may not be designated, but may emerge as a leader in the course of the interaction. It could be close to home—negotiating a family budget, conducting a volunteer meeting, coaching an athletic team. Or it could be on a broader scale—a city-wide organization, a regional or national policy-making body.

Nonviolent leaders are not in it for the glory. Martin Luther King Jr. warned of the desire to stand out ahead of the crowd, to receive the praise and glory that often accompany the front-runner. He called it the "drum major instinct." It's deceptively easy to slide over from bringing out the best in others to using one's position for personal glory. Jesus offered a contrast to the drum major instinct. "Let the greatest among you be as the youngest, and the leader as the servant" (Luke 22:26).

What to Do and How to Do It

Nonviolent leadership involves both the goal and the means to the goal. Both should be in harmony with the basic principles of nonviolence. The goal of any activity in which nonviolent leaders are involved should be life-enhancing, not demeaning. If it's the family budget, some money will be designated to support justice and peace causes. If it's a volunteer meeting, the group will be about the interests of others and not just self-aggrandizing. If it's an athletic team, care will be taken for developing the players and respecting opponents, not just winning games.

A nonviolent leader supports policies that improve the quality of life. He or she does not pander to baser instincts like racial or religious prejudice, economic aggrandizement, cultural anxiety, or the neurotic need to obey authority. Leaders who do such pandering may indeed have appeal, but their cause is not humane and will ultimately be demeaning to themselves and their followers.

Assuming a humane goal, the nonviolent leader employs techniques that enhance the contributions of all. Technical knowledge of the intricacies of the operation is important. Leaders have to know what they're doing, and those they're leading have to be aware of it. But even more than the technical, leaders have to employ productive ways of human interaction.

At the beginning, everyone's guard is up. In successful leadership the cycle of distrust must be broken. We can help make the breakthrough by reaching out in an affirmative, non-threatening way. A nonviolent leader will take the first step, and continue taking it even when it's not initially reciprocated. Nonviolent leadership calls for a significant degree of trust toward those with whom we are working. We have to expect that they will not take advantage of us but will respond in a constructive way. We can help create that atmosphere by showing early and often that our words and actions are intended to be helpful, not harmful.

Working With, Not Over

Nonviolent leadership excludes top-down managerial theory, no matter what its claims for efficiency. Nonviolent leadership is based on the conviction that, because cooperation is a law of our species, people do their best when they're encouraged and assisted, not when they're commanded or intimidated.

"Constructive participation" is the catchword: people working together toward a common humane goal. To encourage this, the nonviolent leader attempts to establish an atmosphere of concern and appreciation. Respect for the participants involves allowing everyone to speak, to express opinions, not imposing ideas even though the leader may be convinced that her or his ideas indeed are the most effective under the circumstances. Encouraging others to contribute can help them clarify their thoughts, adding to the richness of the interaction.

Nonviolent leaders don't allow themselves to be put off by personal characteristics they don't like in others. In a meeting or a group activity some assertive souls may attempt to dominate everyone else. The nonviolent leader's task then may be to reign in the enthusiasm of the few in the interests of enhancing the participation of the many. Respect for all will allow those reticent ones, who prefer to remain quiet, to do so. They are encouraged, but not forced, to contribute. The idea is to bring out all the resources present in the belief that a more sound decision will emerge if everyone is heard than if the ideas of one or just a few dominate the day. And it's also more likely that everyone will own the outcome, and not just go along with whatever decisions are reached.

Because a nonviolent leader's purpose is to reinforce, support, and liberate others, timely silence is important. This frees others to talk, to express feelings, to share ideas. Liberating silence is not just an impatient pause, a polite restraint to give the other a turn until I can jump in again. It's a silence that involves concentrated attention on what the other is saying. It is active, supportive listening.

The effective nonviolent leader will also be aware of the need to move on and get the job done, not placing an inordinate emphasis on the process. Meetings that drag on in the interest of involving everyone past the point of progress are annoying, can waste valuable time, and diminish respect for the facilitator. A nonviolent leader will be aware of creating a common understanding of time in the group, especially if the group has people from different backgrounds, particularly regarding starting and ending times.

The contemporary technique and practice of "Appreciative Inquiry" embodies the qualities of nonviolent leadership. Before jumping into the matter of the moment, time is taken for a (brief) look at past positive results, using these results to take next steps, increase the energy of the group or organization, and make change.

Appreciative Inquiry stresses the talents of all as plans are formulated and encourages constructive participation throughout. It looks at the way human systems function in a more holistic and humanistic manner.[1]

A Bonus

Although athletic coaches are not generally known for their espousal of nonviolence, they may use active nonviolent tactics without considering them as such. The Memphis professional basketball team, the Grizzlies, brought in a new coach during the 2002-2003 season. He was a seventy-year-old man named Hubie Brown, lured out of retirement to bring his expertise and skill to a sport legendary for individualistic performances. He hadn't coached for twenty years. He faced a huge generation gap, being twice as old as the oldest player on the team.

Over the course of his first season he gained everyone's respect by his knowledge of the game. The players came to trust him because he made sure everyone on the team participated to the full extent of their abilities. He gradually instilled in them a selflessness unusual for this sport, a high degree of teamwork pleasing to players and fans alike. The result: in the following season, 2003-2004, the team reached the playoffs for the first time in its history. And he was named Coach of the Year for the entire NBA.

Those of us interested in nonviolent leadership can appreciate the personal qualities and effective techniques of a leader in a sport that has never been, and would not want to be, considered nonviolent.

Nonviolent leadership works better than forcing our way on others or cowing down to them in submission. Active nonviolence turns us outward, away from a self-centered concentration on personal happiness. It increases our sensitivity to the needs of others, reaching out and improving things for *them*. In doing so we find that things improve for ourselves as well.

Part Four

Enemies

The Biblical image of the world is the good but fallen creation. It is good because, as the prophet Jeremiah said, it was made by God's power and established by God's wisdom (Jeremiah 10:12). But because of sin, the world is fallen. The world's wisdom is, in Paul's words, "foolishness in the sight of God" (1 Corinthians 3:19a). Nevertheless there is hope, because "God so loved the world as to give the Only Begotten One" (John 3:16a). And that One, Jesus, told his disciples, "You are the light of the world" (Matthew 5:14a). Those followers of Jesus who have been lights of the world over the ages have acted not according to the wisdom of the world, which is foolishness in the sight of God, but according to a world-defying wisdom. Many of them have brought to the world a transforming beam of nonviolence. Through the patient, persevering shining of active nonviolence in the face of hostility, difficult people, and human brokenness, they are nudging the world in the direction of its created goodness.

Chapter 10

Love Not Like

Jesus didn't say we wouldn't have enemies, or that we shouldn't have any. But he did teach us a better way of reacting to them than retaliating, a better way than fighting to overcome them. His formula is precise: "You have heard that it was said, 'Love your neighbor and hate your enemy.' But I tell you: love your enemies and pray for those who persecute you" (Matthew 5:43-44).

Luke expanded the formula. "I tell you who hear me: Love your enemies, do good to those who hate you, bless those who curse you, pray for those who mistreat you" (Luke 6:27-28). The most productive response to enemies is to build rapport: bless them, pray for them, reach out to them. Enmity brings hurt and destruction. Love brings help and healing.

Jesus did not say, "Like your enemies." His formula doesn't mean that we have to like those who want to or do hurt us. Liking is an emotional response we can't always conjure up. It's feeling good about somebody. Jesus was more realistic than that. His sense of psychology was sound. If we try to stir up pleasant feelings toward somebody who is bent on doing us harm, we waste a lot of psychic energy. So we don't spend time trying to like these people. Nor should we be disappointed when we have unpleasant feelings about them. Dislike and distaste are entirely appropriate toward those who want to hurt us.

Love, according to Aquinas, is an act of the will, not of the emotions. Love is the desire for the good of another, not necessarily *feeling* good about the other. Love is deeper than liking. We can love without liking. What "enemies" are doing makes us feel sad or afraid or bitter. We acknowledge our negative feelings. But we don't allow ourselves to be dominated by them. We rise above them, and try first of all to look at the humanity of our enemy.

It's not a sentimental journey. Love of enemies is not feeling good about them. It is, rather, a purposeful, firm decision to respect them as human beings, to work to resolve our differences through a long process of, as Luke put it, doing good, blessing, praying, and above all, relating to them as having the humanity we have. The immediate goal is to diminish the flare of hostility, keep it from escalating further, calm things. The ultimate goal is that we and they become cooperators in a common effort to improve things for all of us.

Enemy love strikes at the root of hostility. The Latin word for enemy, *inimicus*, is the negative of *amicus*, friend, which is derived from *amare*, to love. Enmity develops from a lack of love. The radical cure for enmity is to put love there.

That Other Cheek

Jesus taught a distinctly active and nonviolent way of reacting to enemies. It's a way that's often been misunderstood as passively giving in. But in reality it's anything but passive. "You have heard that it was said, 'An eye for an eye and a tooth for a tooth.' But I say to you, offer no resistance to one who is evil. When someone strikes you on your right cheek, turn the other one as well. If anyone wants to go to law with you over your tunic, hand over your cloak as well. Should anyone press you into service for one mile, go with him for two" (Matthew 5:38-41).

The original "eye for an eye" in the Hebrew Scriptures was intended to limit retaliation. If someone blackens your eye, it's okay to blacken back, but don't blow off a face or chop off a head. Jesus proposed something entirely different from this limited retaliation. When he said to offer no resistance, he made it clear by his three examples that he meant offer no violent resistance. But what he said to do is definitely resistance, as Scripture scholar Walter Wink has made clear in unpacking the three examples.[1]

Picture the first scene, striking on the cheek. You're face to face with someone who is upset with you. If that person hits you on the right side of your face—and the text does specify the right cheek—it's not going to be a slugging but, as the culture specified using only the right hand (the left was reserved for bathroom functions), an insulting backhand slap, something done to a person of lesser social standing. So what does Jesus teach as the nonviolent response to an insulting backhand slap? Not slapping back, but standing calmly, turning the other cheek as if to say, "Okay, you insulted me. If you want to hit me again, go ahead." But this would mean an open-handed slap on the left cheek, the sign of an equal. The power dynamics are changed.

The second example is a court scene, a lawsuit over a piece of clothing. This would happen to people who were so poor that all they had left were the clothes on their backs. If a plaintiff would go that far, Jesus says, then give the rest of your clothes also, and stand naked in the courtroom. Since nakedness was a cultural shame on the person who saw it and not on the person who was naked, the plaintiff and participants would be shamed and the injustice of the situation exposed.

The final example is pressing into service for a mile. Jesus' listeners would know that he was referring to Roman soldiers demanding that a Judean or Galilean carry their baggage. When a soldier was transferred to another post, he would have to take along his heavy pack, weighing seventy or eighty pounds. It was common practice to commandeer a nearby local to carry the pack. This practice had gotten so out of hand, intensifying opposition to the occupation, that the military command issued a restriction. A soldier could order a civilian to carry his pack, but for no more than a mile. Then he had to get someone else. Jesus said that if someone presses you into that kind of service for a mile, offer to carry the pack a second mile. That nonviolent gesture would catch the soldier off guard. If he accepted the second mile, he could get in trouble. If he didn't accept it because it was against regulations, he might think twice about the kind of people his army was dominating.

Realistic Enemy Love

The love Jesus advocated means persevering through difficult, even painful, experiences. It means not being intimidated by hostility, but trying to reach hostile persons, engaging them in the human interaction necessary to defuse it. The nonviolent way relies on courageous human action. It can move even the most hardened to make concessions to it.

If the other side initially refuses to join in dialogue, we have many avenues of persuasion available, a whole array of nonviolent techniques for bringing about negotiations. The marches and demonstrations of the civil rights movement were designed to bring about negotiations. Creating tension may force attention to the issue. Such tension is positive and creative, exposing injustice.

Once the initial breakthrough is made, the nonviolent process of loving involves a back-and-forth communication to work out a solution both can live with. Dialogue begins when confrontation ends.

Rather than defeat, we want a mutually acceptable solution to our quarrel. It's called win-win. Both sides achieve some of their objectives and are satisfied with the overall results. Seeking a win-win outcome means accepting the partially good intentions of the enemy and working with them. The results will not conform entirely to our preferred blueprint, but the mixture of both sides' assets will endow the end product with a richness that our way alone would not give.

The nonviolent attitude Jesus advocated was spelled out further by Paul in what has been called his Great Pacifist Paragraph: "Bless those who persecute you, bless and do not curse them...Do not repay anyone evil for evil. Be careful to do what is right in the eyes of everybody. If it is possible, as far as it depends on you, live at peace with everyone. Do not take revenge, my friends...On the contrary, if your enemy is hungry, feed your enemy; if thirsty, give something to drink...Do not be overcome by evil, but overcome evil with good" (Romans 12:14, 17-19a, 20a, 21).

Chapter 11

When Others are Difficult

We see anyone who upsets us or causes us grief or anxiety as being difficult at that moment. If it's a passing encounter, we can say goodbye and walk away. But if it's someone we need to live with or work with or associate with over a longer time, then we usually can't just say goodbye and walk away. Sometimes prudence dictates that we should, but it doesn't solve the problem. The person we perceive as difficult is staying around and our differences continue. He or she can generate within us a residue of frustration, a pile of poison that corrodes our sense of well-being and pushes us toward an angry outburst.

Dorothy Day called it "a penance" to endure the pinpricks of living with difficult people. And she had to endure many in the houses of hospitality—those who sought shelter from the streets and sometimes the more permanent members who formed the backbone of the community.

Gandhi himself could be difficult at times. His personal secretary Mahadev Desai once penned, after a particularly frustrating encounter with the Mahatma:

> To live with the saints in heaven
> Is filled with bliss and glory.
> But to live with a saint on earth,
> Well, that's a different story.

My Problem or Theirs

A positive nonviolent approach to difficult people starts out with giving ourselves enough space to figure out why we find them difficult. Sometimes it's my problem. Their particular idiosyncrasies rub me the wrong way. I don't like the way they dress, or talk, or their assertive action. My Shadow is showing. I'm projecting. It's my problem, and I have to deal with it.

But sometimes it's their doing, not mine. They really are trying, deliberately or not, to get under my skin, to provoke me, to make me feel bad with sarcastic remarks, engaging in verbal one-upmanship. Many people are able to gain a sense of adequacy within themselves only when they feel others are inferior. One way to make others inferior is to belittle, to put down verbally, to bully into submission. Many who abuse others were themselves victimized—as children at home or by overly zealous discipline at school or in the military. Because their resentment cannot be directed against the ones who caused their unhappiness, they make someone closer at hand their victim, someone who appears weaker. They are saying, in effect, "I don't feel very good, but I'll be better if you feel worse than I do. So I'm going to make you feel worse."

Overt male chauvinism, an attitude of superiority expressed verbally in ways such as snide remarks about or direct put-downs of women, may often be the result of a long-standing feeling of frustration or doubt about self-worth. Women are seen as more vulnerable and become the object of attack. One man, who admitted he would like to hurt a woman in some way, described his urge: "Just the fact that they can come up to me and just melt me and make me feel like a dummy makes me want revenge...I feel that they have power over me just by their presence...They have power over me so I want power over them."

Step Back

It helps to know all this in theory, but when we're in the presence of a difficult person it's hard to remember in the heat of the moment. Sometimes it's best to take a step back, keep quiet, calm down. Reacting in kind easily aggravates the difficulty.

A cherished relationship can deteriorate when the conduct of one party changes significantly or an aspect of one's personality emerges in an incessantly grating way or a mental condition overflows into psychotic behavior. We try to live with it at first. But when we recognize that we're preoccupied in a harmful, even destructive, way, when we acknowledge that we're becoming listless or bitter, we may have to take that step back. There comes a time, to avoid one or both of us being severely harmed, that we have to break off the relationship, at least temporarily. We withdraw for a while to get a better perspective on what should be done in the short run to deal with the difficulty in the longer run. We get help.

Loving a difficult person nonviolently means first of all putting aside notions of winning. It is especially important, in working it out, to avoid self-righteousness and the kind of moral pressure that humiliates the other side. We recognize their weaknesses, embarrassment, and fears, as we acknowledge our own. Real progress comes from giving the other side options to respond to, not demands to be met. People react poorly to ultimatums. They generally become defensive and hardened in their positions.

Through patient perseverance in loving, not necessarily liking, difficult people we have a good chance of finding a way to live in harmony, respecting their humanity while being true to our own.

Chapter 12

Personal Assault

I used to be able to say I hadn't been mugged. Now I can't say that. It happened one sultry Memphis evening a few years ago. After dinner at home with a friend, Janice and I walked him to his car in the parking area near our apartment. The car was brand-new. Janice got in the driver's seat to give it a closer look.

Two young men sauntered over, young men like many others who lived in our complex. Suddenly one of them said, "Give me your wallet." The other had a gun, a shiny chrome automatic, pointing in our direction. I said I didn't have my wallet with me. Our friend began reaching in his pocket for his. Janice, sitting in the car, heard "wallet," and thought these two young people were just harassing us. She didn't see the gun. She called out from the car, in her best schoolteacher voice, "Go away, stop bothering us, just leave. Right now!" The two men looked at her, startled, glanced back at us as though trying to figure out what to do. Then they turned and ran away as fast as I've ever seen anyone run. The whole event lasted less than a minute.

What Janice had done, in the language of nonviolent response to personal assault, was to "throw a curve." She did something unexpected, for which our assailants were totally unprepared.

Like automobile accidents, fires, tornadoes, hurricanes, and earthquakes, the possibility of personal assault is a fact of life. We are all potential victims of a sudden attack on our persons, our possessions, even our life. Everyone should be prepared to face it.

More Curves

These several people did just the right nonviolent thing at just the right time.

A woman with two children in a disabled car late one night on the New Jersey Turnpike looked up to see a man pointing a gun through her window. He ordered her to let him in the car. Instead of panicking, she looked him in the eye and, like the angry mother she was, commanded, "You put that gun away and get in your car and push me to the service area. *And I mean, right now!*" He was startled. He put the gun in his pocket, went back to his car, did as she ordered, pushed her car to the service area, then drove away.[1]

A friend of mine, a large-statured peace activist, walking on a sidewalk in a small town in broad daylight, was suddenly faced with a smaller man flashing a knife and demanding money. The peace person, who had very little money anyway, said that the first thing he thought of was the incongruity of their sizes. "All I could do was laugh," he said. He didn't feel any fear, although later he said he was surprised he hadn't. His self-confidence was deep. The assailant glanced up at him, looked puzzled, then turned and ran away.

One morning a young woman was returning to her car in a library parking garage. A man who appeared pleasant approached and said hello. She nodded back. She was just about to open her car door when he grabbed her arm roughly. She immediately shook him off, looked at him squarely, and said, "You gotta be kidding." He was startled and let go. She quickly got in and locked the door. He looked at her for a moment, then walked away. Her sense of personal power was so strong that it overrode her fear. She reacted in a way that was natural to her but unexpected to her assailant. He was thrown off guard, and she was safe.

Flight or Fight—Not

A police lieutenant who runs clinics on how to cope with rape gives this advice to women. "First, try to escape, or scare away the assailant by wrenching free or yelling. If the criminal doesn't let go, then you have to either give in, or hurt him in the most effective and efficient manner possible." This means, he said, gouge out an eye. Kick hard at the groin. Shoot, if you have a gun, and shoot to kill.

We are all faced with the possibility of being subject to assault. I prefer to say "subject to" rather than "victim of" assault because there is much we can do to keep the encounter from escalating into physical harm. The police officer's advice has a point for people not sensitive to nonviolence or not practiced in its ways. Essentially he is offering the two traditional modes of survival in time of danger: flight or fight. But if we believe in the power of nonviolence, we need to explore how we can respond successfully in this most critical of all personal dangers.

We are not helping ourselves by naively thinking that everything will be all right all the time. It is very nonviolent, not to mention practical, to do everything we reasonably can to avoid being attacked in the first place. That includes locking doors, walking with others rather than alone, avoiding high-risk areas, being alert to potential danger wherever we are. We have to be, as Jesus said, "shrewd as serpents" while being at the same time "innocent as doves" (Matthew 10:16). Safety precautions send a strong signal to anyone who would do us harm that we are alert and prepared to take care of ourselves. For a person tuned in to nonviolence, prevention is not being cowardly, but realistic.

If we sense that an attack is coming, the first nonviolent response is to avoid it. Seek cover. Yes, flight. One woman who was at the scene when a gunman began firing a rifle at marketplace strollers, killing sixteen people, said she survived because she "dove for cover." At critical times like an impending attack we, too, would do well to dive for cover.

We need feel no compunction about it. Jesus himself frequently took evasive action to avoid being hurt. One time after a confrontation with some of his adversaries, "They picked up stones to stone him...Jesus hid himself, slipping away" (John 8:59). That was a way of "diving for cover." Another time, right after John the Baptist was killed, "When Jesus heard what had happened, he withdrew by boat privately to a solitary place" (Matthew 14:13a). He got out of there. He could feel the heat and knew that his time had not yet come.

When Jesus sensed danger he hid out, tried to evade it without giving up his commitment. He advised his disciples to do the same thing. "When you are persecuted in one place, flee to another" (Matthew 10:23a). Stay away from troublesome areas. Don't make yourself an easy mark. That's what he did when he withdrew to the Garden of Olives after the Last Supper, until his hiding place was betrayed by one of his friends.

Self-Possession

As a remote preparation before any attack occurs, we can sharpen our ability for an effective nonviolent response by increasing the power of our personhood. We believe that we are important, we are valuable, and we want others to believe it about us, too. We are not victims, we are not cowering and cringing before life's challenges, fearfully looking over our shoulders to see what might be pursuing us. We stand straight, eyes calm and alert, moving ahead. We walk confidently, in a straightforward and open manner. We are not rash or brash; we don't take unnecessary risks; we're not blind to danger. We are who we are, and we present ourselves that way to the world.

Two strange men entered my wife Janice's aerobics class and began talking loudly, distracting the exercisers. No one knew what they wanted, but they seemed capable of creating trouble. One of the exercisers went over to speak to them. He told them quietly how serious the class was, and that anyone who wanted to take part had to sign a waiver form and pay a fee. They were welcome to join if they wanted. He didn't accuse or threaten; he just spoke straightforwardly, matter-of-factly. They listened, saw his seriousness, then turned away and left. No trouble. It was an exercise in self-possession.

The caricature of the swaggering sheriff with a pistol strapped to one side, a heavy flashlight on the other, a truncheon dangling from his belt, so loaded down that he walks with his elbows pointed outward, is the image of a fearful man who needs all this hardware to protect himself. Given the climate, he has reason to be protective. But his greatest asset is his authority, not his hardware. Until recently, police in London never carried guns. Their training and self-possession were defense enough. And they're usually still enough, even with the discrete pistols they now carry.

Superior Weapons

In principle, people committed to nonviolence don't arm themselves. True, it's because we believe in *ahimsa*, non-harm. But it is also because we believe that, in a crisis, our personal ability is more effective than a gun. Our weapons are the ones described by Paul as the "armor of God": "Stand firm, then, with the belt of truth buckled around your waist, with the breastplate of righteousness in place, and with your feet fitted with the readiness that comes from the gospel of peace" (Ephesians 6:14-15).

Truth, righteousness, and readiness are powerful nonviolent weapons. Armed with them, our personal power increases. These, more than guns and knives, have a deterrent effect on a would-be attacker. Think of a robber lurking in a doorway late at night watching potential marks approaching down the street. The assailant will want to pick out one who looks like an easy victim, timid, uncertain, fearful, unprotected. Someone who appears in command, confident, alert, will not be as appealing a target. If I carry myself this way, I'm likely to be passed over in favor of an easier target—and I'll probably never know how close I came to being attacked.

If a confrontation does occur, this kind of self-possession, this confidence in our nonviolent armor, is the foundation of our defense. But it's only the foundation. An understanding of what is likely to happen, and the consistent practice of nonviolent techniques in other areas of life, can give us an effective response to personal assault.

Easy Does It

Those who have adopted an active nonviolent approach to life are likely in a much better emotional state than the assailant. Still, our first response will probably be a quick flash of fear. We are confronted with a threat, a forceful presence, a fearsome expression, a total stranger suddenly invading our vulnerable space, demanding that we do something extremely unpleasant. We may be hurt or even killed.

We know we have to be very careful. We can't appear to stall, or be cute, or frustrate the attacker, who is bound to be edgy and in a hurry. If we're schooled in nonviolence, our mind will tell us that the attacker, unless insane or under the influence of drugs, is capable of a human response to human overtures. Our mind and training will also tell us that it is precisely in making these overtures, guided by a sense of our own self-worth and personal power, that we have a chance for an effective reaction.

We may not have a chance to do much at all. The attacker could be in such a hurry, in the grips of another fear, that it's over almost before we know what hit us. But most probably we will have some opportunity for interaction. Our aim is to show respect for the attacker as a person. We do nothing threatening. We don't fight back. The attacker is prepared for that. That's the purpose of the knife or gun, or the surprise jump out of the dark, to overpower me and prevent my doing anything to defend myself.

We don't fight back, but at the same time we refuse to cooperate in the attack. The key is to remain calm, to make no sudden moves. It will help to look the person in the eye to pick up some clues, to size up the situation as quickly as possible, almost intuitively. We try to interact personally with the attacker.

One woman, who woke suddenly in the middle of the night to find a strange man at the foot of her bed, reacted in a way totally unexpected to both the intruder and herself. In an instant there flashed before her mind all the things she should not do—scream, beg for mercy, reach for something with which to ward him off, jump out of bed and try to run. She sat up, looked at his dark form, and asked quietly, "What time is it?" He was taken aback, didn't know what to do. Almost reflexively he looked at his watch, and said, "It's three o'clock." She replied, "That's funny, my clock says it's three-fifteen. Do you think your watch could be off?" They had this absurd conversation about whose timepiece was more accurate. And she knew right then that the spell was broken; he was reacting to her as a human being and not as a victim.

Doing the unexpected like that is what Richard Gregg, one of the early U.S. theoreticians of Gandhian nonviolence, called "moral jiu-jitsu." The nonviolence and good will of the potential victim are used in the same way that the lack of physical opposition by the user of physical jiu-jitsu does, causing the attacker to lose what Gregg called "moral balance." The attacker at the foot of the bed had expected resistance, but found none. Instead he responded intuitively to the simple question about what time it was. The potential victim had "thrown a curve."

There's no formula for moral jiu-jitsu. It comes from our reservoir of nonviolent responses in other situations and from our principled decision to be nonviolent in all aspects of life. When we understand the dynamics of a nonviolent response, see how it can work, and above all know some for whom it has worked, we have a better appreciation of its power for our own lives if we are ever faced with the awesome challenge of assault.

Not Just Lucky

When I shared stories like these at a workshop, one woman said of those who had successfully evaded the attacks, "They were just lucky." She was right in one way. They were lucky in hitting on just the right thing to say, just the right look or movement, and they met just the right susceptibility in the attackers. They were lucky to get out of it alive and intact.

But they were not "just" lucky. They were lucky in the same way that a soldier who survives combat is lucky. The bullets didn't find him; he managed not to trip any land mines; when the bombs fell and the shells exploded he found protective cover. But the soldier had increased his chances of surviving through rigorous training. He had learned to discipline himself, not to panic, to rely on the protection of his unit, to improvise under fire. He was lucky to survive. But if he hadn't been trained, he might not have been lucky.

The same is true with a nonviolent response to assault. Any time we get through it without damage we're lucky. But we increase our chances for a good outcome by training ourselves, by studying and practicing what to say and how to act in other, less drastic encounters with difficult people.

Another young participant in a nonviolence training workshop had a different reaction: "This is such a relief. I've been to those sessions where the police showed us how to defend against rape, and I came away really upset. I was afraid it might happen to me, and I know I couldn't gouge out someone's eyes if it did. Now I can see that there are all kinds of different things that I can do, nonviolently. And I don't feel so afraid any more."

Of course, a nonviolent response, even with the personal power of self-possession and skills honed through long practice, doesn't always work. But neither does a violent response. In choosing to defend ourselves nonviolently, we take a risk. But there is a risk in whatever we do when faced with assault. A positive, nonviolent response has at least as much, and probably more, chance of successfully evading an assault than a violent response does.

We know that in the act of assault attackers themselves are afraid. They have no idea what their intended victim will do, whether there is a weapon for defense or a magic whistle to summon immediate assistance. They may act tough, authoritative, demanding, in charge, supported by their weaponry. But inside, they may be hurting, and they are fearful. It takes confidence on our part to believe this of someone about to assault us. We have to go beyond appearances, like knowing the earth is round no matter how flat it looks.

While it is certainly not healthy for us to be assaulted, it is also not healthy either for the one who would perpetrate the assault. In responding nonviolently we try not only to prevent it from happening to ourselves, we also want to prevent the other from committing it. The positive steps we take nonviolently are for our own good, but they are also for the good of the attacker.

And we have a specific Gospel motivation for taking them, what Paul called "the mind of Christ" (1 Corinthians 2:16). That "mind," that attitude, was clearly expressed in his law of love, and particularly in the most demanding clause of that law: love of enemies, including those who would do us damage through assault.

Part Five

Challenges

The Biblical letter attributed to the apostle Peter contains this alert: "Be sober. Be watchful. For your adversary the Devil roams about like a roaring lion seeking someone to devour" (1 Peter 5:8). Whether the challenges put before us come from a human-like evil spirit who is the spiritual adversary of God, or whether they seem like that because they're serious and dangerous, those of us who would be personally nonviolent have to be on our toes—sober, watchful, as Peter says. Some of the challenges are internal, some external. Here we consider three: a debilitating attitude, the ever-pressing problem of money, and the very real desire for revenge.

Chapter 13

Bad Faith

Jean-Paul Sarte used the disturbing image of "bad faith" for efforts to avoid facing unpleasant realities. Everyone experiences unpleasant realities, the ordinary sadness that dots our days—a friend hospitalized, a car breakdown, humiliation after a mistake, a nagging back pain, rumors of job layoffs, the effects of racism. On top of that we are deluged by news about violence, hatred, suffering, greed. We read about banking scandals among the business elite and deliberate deception by government leaders. We hear of another genocide and an AIDS epidemic in Africa.

Some desensitization is imperative to maintain our mental balance and avoid being overwhelmed by so much bleakness. Taking a breather is not bad faith.

What Sartre was talking about is different. It's the deliberate refusal to acknowledge the human suffering that one's actions bring about. Like gun manufacturers. Or cigarette producers. They have to avoid thinking about maimed bodies or cancerous lungs if they're going to do their job well. Or like some in the military who deliberately avoid international news because, as one person said, "If we're ordered to go in someplace and do a job, I don't want to know anything about the people we'll be shooting at."

When the results are painful to face, many just don't want to know about them. It's a lot easier to maintain one's emotional balance by pretending that all's going well, displaying what Martin Luther King Jr. called a "superficial optimism."

It's comforting to minimize the destructiveness in human affairs, to think things will straighten out eventually, that schools will improve, that starvation in sub-Saharan Africa isn't really that bad, or that the air strikes against terrorist hideouts don't really kill innocent people. It's comforting to tell ourselves to wait for more facts, to refuse to react until we have the complete picture. Sartre would label it bad faith.

Good Faith

In contrast to these avoidance mechanisms, Sartre proposed "good faith" as the more difficult but more authentically human response. Good faith is having the courage to face problems, facts, and realities squarely and acknowledge them honestly. Good faith means making the constant effort to learn the truth about ourselves, about our world, and about our selves-in-the-world.

A fundamental truth about ourselves is that we are a mixed collection of good and bad components of gifts and shadows. In Israel Charny's words, "Human beings are at one and the same time beautiful, generous, creative creatures and deadly genociders." A fundamental truth about our world is that it contains, he said, "both a glorious epic of achievements and love and a dreadful blood-soaked nightmare of destruction." A fundamental truth about our selves-in-the-world is that we have the capacity to take part both in the glorious achievements and also in the blood-soaked destruction. A U.S. military man involved in the Abu Ghraib prison abuse during the war against Iraq acknowledged, "The Christian in me says it's wrong, but the corrections officer in me says I love to make a grown man [abuse] himself."

It's hard to shine an exploratory light into our Shadows. It's hard to begin to untangle the subtle web of complexes we have built up to weather the slings and arrows of whatever fortunes and misfortunes we have to face. "Know thyself" was Socrates's challenge for a lifetime.

Today we must add "know thy world" as a lifetime challenge. Searching through historical upheavals, ancient prejudices, and modern machinations for a complete picture is hard, but it's part of good faith. For those of us who are fortunate in our life circumstances, it's easier not to have to look at pictures of starving children or huddled refugees from a besieged village. It's easier to go a few blocks out of the way to avoid seeing the faces outside the homeless mission.

Good faith is the result of an inner decision to come down on the side of reality, no matter how unpleasant it might be. Making this choice involves letting go of the comfort of ignorance. As has been said, "You shall know the truth, and the truth shall make you miserable."

Society both hinders and helps our efforts to know the truth, to face the facts. On the one hand it conditions us to defer to authority, leading to the easy abdication of responsibility to those who are running the government. But at the same time it encourages the quest for knowledge, the curiosity and exploration that can lead to an uncovering of flawed motives, damaging actions, and horrendous consequences.

Such eyes-open awareness is a bitter pill to swallow. Buddhists know it as the First Noble Truth, that all of life involves *dukkha*—the pain and suffering that inevitably mar life. Although unpleasant to contemplate and disquieting to experience, it's an essential element of human wholeness. We have to pop this bitter pill if we would be whole human beings, responsible for the integrity of our lives, and responsible, too, for not contributing to as well as helping to end misery in human lives and the world.

Part of the pain of good faith comes when we face the facts squarely, then respond to them in a way that's different from others of equally good faith. Good people, acting in good faith, can differ seriously with each other. Many are strongly opposed to abortion and press for legislation outlawing it. Many others, with equally good faith, are in favor of a woman's right to make this agonizing personal choice without being treated as a criminal. Many in good faith oppose the use of violence, and advocate conscientious objection to military service, strict gun control, and abolition of capital punishment. Many others, in equally good faith, favor the use of violence to defend themselves, their families, their property, and their country. Both are facing the same realities, but differ in their approaches to the solutions.

Because it's often painful, our stretching toward good faith requires inner strength to face appalling facts when they appear. Most of us, in struggle, will only partially achieve a good faith response to the mixed-up world of our time. The degree of good faith we achieve may not solve the world's problems, but it will nudge us toward actions that help rather than harm, actions that contribute to human relief rather than human suffering.

Chapter 14

Mammon

The word "money" is neutral. "Mammon" is not. It has a distinctly unpleasant overtone. The word means the kind of wealth that has a debasing effect. Although it is never found in the Hebrew Scriptures and rarely in the New Testament, when it does show up, it shows up as something negative. Jesus said, "You cannot serve God and mammon" (Matthew 6:24a).

In trying to be nonviolent toward ourselves we need to take a look at the challenge posed by this omnipresent, omnipressing reality called money, which all too easily can take the form of mammon.

Because the national economy is geared to expanding production, we are all bombarded to buy, regardless of our means, regardless also of real need. Too many get entangled in unnecessary debt, juggling credit card accounts, looking ahead to the next paycheck, always needing just a little more to make ends meet. "I owe, I owe, it's off to work I go," a bumper sticker proclaimed.

The sheer abundance in department stores is overwhelming, gagging. If I spend more than a short time in any of them, I feel woozy, off-balance. I experience sensory overload. On one level I want what I see, and at the same time, I want not to want it. And there's too much there to want anyway. I'm dazed.

It's ironic, but appropriate, that the National Product is called "Gross."

Constant decisions about money are thrust on us. If we don't have it, how can we get enough to survive? If a modest amount is flowing through our life so that we can put some aside, how much should we save? For what? How much should we give away? To whom? We find ourselves, like it or not, devoting considerable attention to money. If we don't serve it as our ultimate concern, we can easily find ourselves bogged down in servicing it by balancing the checkbook, stretching the paycheck, prioritizing the bills, figuring how to save something, attending to payment deadlines.

Dangerous Money

Because the Kindom has not yet fully come and we have to live in this world while trying not to be thoroughly *of* it, we have to come to grips with money. The New Testament puts a big "hazardous material" stamp on it. Early Christians believed that "the love of money is the root of all evils" (1 Timothy 6:10a). Jesus' assessment is to handle with care. He said, "Take care to guard against all greed, for though one may be rich, one's life does not consist of possessions" (Luke 12:15).

The way Jesus spoke about money rings a bell with anyone tuned in to nonviolence. Money and all personal possessions can be mental and emotional, not to mention spiritual, traps. Look out. Money can grab us and take over our lives. That's why it is "easier for a camel to go through the eye of a needle than for a rich person to enter the Kindom of God" (Matthew 19:24). Some would seek wiggle room by saying that the "eye of a needle" referred to a small opening in Jerusalem's wall and therefore a camel could squeeze through—a tiny camel, a little money, extremely difficult in either case.

And yet, a few verses later Jesus held out some hope. "But with God all things are possible" (Matthew 19:26b). How is God going to pull off this trick of getting a camel through the eye of a needle? Enlarge the needle? Reduce the size of the camel? I think God is going to do it by encouraging wealthy people to become less wealthy in a hurry. You've been gifted, okay, use it for others who haven't been so gifted. To a rich young man Jesus said, "Go, sell what you have and give to the poor, and you will have treasure in heaven" (Mark 10:21b). Make sure your money is used to benefit those in need.

I don't take Jesus' words to the rich young man as an absolute injunction to divest of everything and become one of the wretched of the earth myself. That is incompatible with the rest of his teaching about the character of the Kindom. I take his words as advice on the responsible use of one's resources. Jesus was speaking to a *rich* young man, who could afford to give much away to others.

Neither Poverty nor Luxury

Looking with a nonviolent eye at the economic spectrum, we can be sure that the poverty at one end is not good. It's not right when a person doesn't have enough to eat, a place to sleep, can't get medical treatment, doesn't have a job, where survival is a problem every day. This kind of poverty is not a characteristic of the Reign of God where the hungry will be fed, the naked clothed, the homeless sheltered. We help to bring about this Kindom by following Jesus' suggestions. Share with others. If someone is hungry, feed the person. Make people less poor. Poverty, a degradation of the human condition, is something to be eliminated. No one should be that poor.

Luxury, superfluity, at the other end of the economic spectrum is not right either, because of the selfishness it inevitably involves and the good use to which it could otherwise be put. Not enough has been given away; it has been held too tightly, grasped too closely. It makes its owners prisoners of their possessions, what George Carlin called their "stuff." When this happens the money of luxury has become mammon.

Jesus told the story about a rich man "who was dressed in purple and fine linen and lived in luxury every day." The story's other character is a beggar named Lazarus, "covered with sores and longing to eat what fell from the rich man's table." The poor man died and went to heaven. When the rich man died, "in hell, where he was in torment, he looked up and saw...Lazarus" in heaven (from Luke 16:19-23). Jesus didn't say why the rich man went to hell. The implication, though, is that, living in luxury, he ignored the beggar at his gate and that he could only maintain his luxury at the expense of others.

There's a large area between the extreme of poverty and the extreme of luxury. I think of that middle ground as "decency." Somewhere in the area of decency is where people who would be nonviolent can, with integrity, locate themselves. Decency means that our basic needs of food, clothing, and shelter are met, education and health care are available, and we have opportunities for enriching ourselves with spiritual, cultural, and recreational experiences. Decency is not always easy to delineate. It can't be pinpointed with accuracy, and it varies from culture to culture.

Some decide to live toward the lower end and choose an existence with less material wealth. They see it as a way of identifying more closely with those who are oppressed, who are forced to be poor. Or they want to restrict their income so they won't have to pay taxes that maintain structures of violence. Or they believe in conserving the world's resources in the interest of a more equitable distribution. They try to live simply so that others may simply live. And they can find it liberating.

Others, equally concerned, do not feel called to that lower end, wanting to be relatively free from preoccupation about marginal housing or medical insurance or their children's education. They believe they can more effectively work for the Kindom if they themselves have sufficient resources to cope with life's challenges and help others up from the poverty in which they have been entrenched.

A nonviolent response to money's danger is to be carefully restrained around it. The Chinese sage Lao Tzu said, "To take all you want is never as good as to stop when you should." Gandhi was even more emphatic: "Civilization, in the real sense of the term, consists not in the multiplication, but in the deliberate and voluntary reduction of wants." And therefore, he thought, "we must keep the ideal constantly in view, and in the light thereof, critically examine our possessions and try to reduce them."

A nonviolent attitude toward money calls for constant vigilance over our desires, constant discernment about whether something is necessary or superfluous. A nonviolent approach to money calls for us to be in a reduction mode rather than an acquisition mode. What we do with our money is a signal of what our lives are all about, what we are. "For where your treasure is, there also will your heart be" (Matthew 6:21). The responsible direction of our life is at stake in the responsible use of our money.

Chapter 15

Revenge

Desire for revenge is a natural reaction. It feels good to get even. We recognize it in the outrage of an Iraqi mob in Fallujah who bombed a car of people from the United States and then dragged their bodies out and mutilated them. We recognize it in the intense hostility of a crowd of Nicaraguans shortly after the fall of the Somoza regime in 1979. Several of the infamous *Guardia Nacional* had been captured and were detained in the Red Cross building in Managua. An angry crowd gathered outside and began pounding on the doors shouting for the murderers to be brought outside for lynching.

We may sympathize with the resisters to the U.S. occupation in Iraq, or the crowd who wanted to lynch the Nicaraguan guardsmen.

Gandhi showed us a different way of getting even. When he was in prison in South Africa, he made a pair of sandals and later presented them as a gift to the official responsible for putting him there, General Jan Christian Smuts. Years later General Smuts said he had been touched by the gift, that it had helped change his attitude toward Gandhi. "I have worn them for many a summer since then," he said, "even though I may feel I am not worthy to stand in the shoes of so great a man."

In Nicaragua an official also showed a different way to the angry crowd in Managua. Tomás Borge, the new Minister of the Interior, heard the uproar and hurried over to the scene. He said later that if he had wanted to please them—not just those who were there, but others whose family members had been brutally killed by the *Guardia*—he would have ordered the prisoners executed. Instead, he confronted the angry shouters and demanded that they stop: "We cannot kill these men, because we carried out this revolution in order to bring an end to massacres. What's the purpose of it if we're just going to repeat what they did? In that case we would be better off never having undertaken this revolution!" The crowd quieted down and slowly disbanded. Instead of revenge, they would begin to build a society based on humane values, not dictatorial force.[1]

Those Burning Coals

The apostle Paul also taught a different way. Break the cycle, he wrote. "Do not repay anyone evil for evil" (Romans 12:17a). Do something different. In giving food or drink or making some other positive gesture to those who have offended, we "heap burning coals on their heads" (Romans 12:20b). Burning coals sounds jarringly different from what we think of as the nonviolent ideal. They are a feeling of shame that can occur when oppressors come to recognize their wrong direction and begin to back off.

It takes vision and courage to react to an insult in a positive, nonviolent way. Paul had both. He was not only fearless in the face of hostility, he was often able to turn the tables on those who opposed him. Once, when he and Silas ran into trouble in Philippi, the city authorities "ordered them to be stripped and beaten. After they had been severely flogged, they were thrown into prison, and the jailer was commanded to guard them carefully. Upon receiving such orders, he put them in the inner cell and fastened their feet in the stocks" (Acts of the Apostles 16:22b-24).

Paul resented this unjust treatment. Had he made a gesture of getting even later when he had the chance, we would have understood. And he did have the chance. In the middle of the night escape suddenly became possible.

> Suddenly there was such a violent earthquake that the foundations of the prison were shaken. At once all the prison doors flew open, and everybody's chains were loose. The jailer woke up, and when he saw the prison doors open, he drew his sword and was about to kill himself because he thought the pri-

soners had escaped. But Paul shouted, "Don't harm yourself! We are all here." The jailer called for lights, rushed in and fell trembling before Paul and Silas (Acts 16:26-29).

Instead of getting even when he had the chance, Paul's response was nonviolent. He took time to console and reach out to the jailer. A few hours later the city magistrates ordered the prisoners released. But Paul and Silas didn't slip away quietly. Paul called the city officials to task. He wanted them to see the problem they had created in treating Silas and him so abusively. He demanded that these city officials escort them from the prison in person, thereby publicly acknowledging their mistake. And they did (Acts 16:39)! Paul's "revenge" on these city officials was getting them to accompany Silas and him personally and apologetically from the very prison to which they had expeditiously assigned them the day before.

Don't get mad, get even, runs conventional wisdom. Gandhi knew that returning violence for violence, hatred for hatred, only multiplies trouble. "An eye for an eye leaves the whole world blind," he said. It gives the cycle of unpleasantness another push, and everybody feels worse in the long run. These kinds of behaviors are what a Hebrew prophet called sowing the wind and reaping the whirlwind (Hosea 8:7).

It takes courage and imagination to even the score in a nonviolent way, as Paul did in Philippi, as Gandhi did by making the sandals, as Tomás Borge did by calming the call for retribution. And it's far, far better than the alternative.

Part Six

Understanding and Facing Empire

"No one can serve two masters," Jesus said. "You will either hate one and love the other, or be attentive to one and despise the other" (Matthew 6:24). We cannot be on the side of truth and goodness and at the same time support those forces that would set brother against brother, sister against sister, country against country. Our nonviolence takes two forms—a firm no to those who propel us on the road of killing, injustice, and destruction and a strong yes to constructive means to resolve conflicts and problems on the personal, social, and international levels. Our firm no means we are not with those who wage pre-emptive war, support and continue injustice of all forms, and develop weapons of genocide and terror. Our strong yes signals our stand on the side of all who work for dignity and justice, who oppose war, who want to dismantle weapons of genocide and terror, who are on the wrong side of power.

A large measure of the world's power and greed has been concentrated in the empires that have dotted its history. To act nonviolently in its face, we have to know its features, the dynamics of empire, as well as how nationalism plays out. And we have to know what to do with the anger we feel at the abuses of empire and other injustices.

Chapter 16

Empire

No sooner had the old thirteen colonies become the new United States than an even more grandiose vision of the future appeared. Benjamin Franklin celebrated the new nation as the dawn of a new empire which, he felt, would enjoy divine approval. Alluding to a saying of Jesus in the Gospel of Matthew (10:29), Franklin stated, "If a sparrow cannot fall to the ground without His notice, is it probable that an empire can arise without His aid?" Franklin's sparrow came from Jesus. The empire part was his own.

With or without divine aid, the fledgling nation plunged full-speed ahead with imperial ambitions. White settlers moved westward and took over lands of native peoples. By the Monroe Doctrine of 1823, only forty years after the end of the Revolutionary War, the United States warned European powers not to intervene in the Americas. Like imperial Rome which had treated the Mediterranean as *mare nostrum*, "our sea," the United States over the next two centuries treated Central and South America as "our continent."

From Sea to Shining Sea—and Beyond

When the United States defeated Spain in 1898 it reached into the Pacific and took over the Philippines and Guam and into the Atlantic for Cuba and Puerto Rico. It turned Cuba into its playground until Fidel Castro claimed its full independence a half century later. Puerto Rico's citizens cannot vote in U.S. elections, but can be conscripted into the U.S. military. After a brutal war against Philippine insurrectionists, the United States finally gave the country back to its own people. Everything else was kept, and the United States added a few more, like American Samoa and the

Mariannas.

The United States bought Alaska from Russia in 1867 and the Virgin Islands from Denmark in 1917. U.S. companies moved to Hawaii for its sugar and pineapples and the islands were "annexed" in 1898, long before it became the 50th state in 1959. The United States engineered Panama's independence from Colombia, then in a gunboat treaty in 1903 took possession of a strip across its middle to build an ocean-connecting canal. The United States held on to that strip for three-quarters of a century before agreeing in 1977 to withdraw by the end of the century.

Although most U.S. citizens shy away today from calling these far-flung outposts of empire colonies (a preferred term is "outlying areas"), Guam says it's "where America's day begins."

In Iraq in 2003 the United States not only toppled a dictator, but made it clear it intended to run the country a long way into the future. U.S. people were in charge, operating out of the largest embassy in the world, no matter how it was covered over with the fig leaf the U.S. administration called "sovereignty." Rebuilding the infrastructure was put in the hands of U.S. corporations or of international businesses approved by the U.S. government. The United States wanted to control Iraq for its oil, of course, and also for its strategic location to facilitate U.S. influence throughout the whole Middle East. Oil for U.S. machinery, location for U.S. commerce.

Good for Business

More than two centuries ago, Adam Smith, in his *Wealth of Nations*, wrote that founding a great empire is a project "extremely fit for a nation whose government is influenced by shopkeepers" (today read "free trade capitalists"). "Such statesmen, and such statesmen only," Smith continued, "are capable of fancying that they will find some advantage in employing the blood and treasure of their fellow-citizens to found and maintain such an empire."[1]

The United States has employed considerable blood and treasure of its citizens over the years to found, enlarge, and defend its far-flung "outlying areas" and move into new ones, like Iraq. In doing so it has followed in the footsteps of other recent empires of shopkeepers, notably the British and the French.

The British, on whose empire at one point in time the sun never set, controlled the whole subcontinent of India as well as large territories in Africa and the Middle East, including Iraq after the First World War. The French, a century after Napoleon's short-lived imperial adventures, vied with Britain for the rest of Africa and the Middle East. They also controlled southeast Asia, where the United States moved in after they pulled out.

Force and Fear

To defend its rising empire, the United States has long acquired the best and most powerful weapons money and talent could produce, justifying its own weapons of mass destruction as necessary for defense, while repudiating the same justification for other countries. Empire calls for constantly expanding and upgrad-ing destructive capability, including a nuclear arsenal which con-tinues to threaten human catastrophe. The process has been wrapped in the flag and packaged as national security. President George W. Bush argued that "we" will do anything to "defend our way of life."

What we're not told is that the United States wants those people and lands out there for their raw materials and for their markets. It all goes with an empire. For most of the rest of the world it is, in Jonathan Schell's prophetic words, "something to rebel against." The Indian writer Arundhati Roy has said, "Debating imperialism is like arguing the pros and cons of rape." From her perspective in the developing world the United States appears not just as one empire among others whose shipwrecks are dotted through history, but as a unique world dominator. "For the first time in history, a single Empire with an arsenal of weapons that could obliterate the world in an afternoon has complete, unipolar, economic and military hegemony...There isn't a country on God's earth that is not caught in the cross hairs of American cruise missiles and the IMF chequebook."[2]

The current label for those who oppose the United States is

"terrorists." And there is a war against them, a unilaterally declared "war against terror." And it's going to go on for a long, long time. The Defense Secretary, Donald Rumsfeld, told the 2004 graduating class at the United States Military Academy at West Point: "We are closer to the beginning of this struggle, this global insurgency, than to its end."

The war against terror is really a war for empire—a war to maintain it, a war to expand it. It helps stifle internal dissent if U.S. citizens can be made suspicious not only of everyone else in the world, but also of each other. "If you're not with us, you're with the terrorists," President George W. Bush has said. Fear now extends to internal suspicion, fear of neighbors, personal profiling, communication monitoring, and suspicious behavior reporting, all made legal and wrapped in the flag by a piece of lengthy legislation with the unwieldy title "Uniting and Strengthening America by Providing Appropriate Tools Required to Intercept and Obstruct Terrorism," better known by its initials as the USA PATRIOT Act.

Another View

Those who follow the teachings of national administrations look on the U.S. empire with pride. Those who follow the teachings of Jesus are called to something quite different. "You know that those who are recognized as rulers over the Gentiles lord it over them, and their great ones make their authority felt over them. But it shall not be so among you. Rather, whoever wishes to be great among you will be your servant" (Mark 10:42-43). Not authority over, he said, but service to. Not the U.S. way of imperial control, but the Biblical way of servant leadership.

The root of the word empire is the Latin *imperium*, meaning "absolute authority." Any empire, the United States included, involves absolute power at home and abroad. This kind of power has dangerous consequences—physical yes, but even more important, spiritual. The British historian Lord Acton long ago warned, "Power tends to corrupt; absolute power corrupts absolutely." He was in a position to know, living in the heart of the British empire.

Those who cheer the expansion of the U.S. empire, and even

dare to believe it has divine approval, may not want to face its endless wars and its corrupting power. They may not want to face empire's seeds of hatred, its rebellions, and its ultimate consequences. As Jesus put it, "What profit is there to gain the whole world and lose or forfeit one's self?" (Luke 9:25)—meaning one's inner identity, one's soul. When we look at it that way, the outcome is clear: support empire, lose soul.

Chapter 17

Group Narcissism: Nationalism

We have no programmed pattern in our genetic makeup to kill other human beings. If we did, we would all be killers, and we're not. We might kill out of self-defense, or in an aggressive outburst, or in cold-blooded revenge or intimidation. But none of this is instinctual. It's learned. It's a pattern of behavior that is socially acceptable and culturally encouraged. If killing is not in our genes, something else is—the need to feel part of a reality greater than ourselves.

To compensate for weakness and insecurity, many look to their ethnic group or religion or nation for support. They're "my people," and I'm proud to be part of them. This can have positive results, such as protection from physical and psychological damage or pride in one's heritage. But allegiance to "my people" can become especially dangerous when it takes the form of what Erich Fromm called "group narcissism." That's when I look on "my people" as superior to others, maybe even the greatest, the best, the most noble. "We're Number One." Any one of us may not be the best. But our group is, or our country is, and we're part of it.

Nationalism

Instead of understanding one's country in the context of a community of nations, group narcissism elevates it above that world community, refusing to acknowledge that its true welfare has to include respect for the rights of others. Group narcissism in the form of nationalism is especially potent because many nations have very powerful weapons (including economic ones) and can inflict great harm. When people are more uncertain than confident, more fearful of their failures than secure in their accomplishments, they tend to push hard to assert themselves, especially when a threat is perceived. Group narcissism elevates one's country above other moral concerns. "I'll not only die for my country, but I'll kill for it."

National self-admiration waxes strong in the face of outsiders, who often become enemies. George Kennan observed, "We seem to have to feel we need to reassure ourselves constantly of how fine we are, how virtuous we are, how wonderful we are. And for that we need some other country that is exactly the opposite." So we, as a group representing a country, have frequently located an enemy and been ready to fight, to prove ourselves. We'll show ourselves how good we are by standing up against that enemy.

Barbara Ehrenreich, in *Blood Rites: Origins and History of the Passions of War*, pointed out that our ancestors in the distant past may have had to band together to ward off predator animals. But that time has long since passed. Now, in the artificial constructs called nations, people band together against outside threats, whether real or trumped-up.

Leaders of nations almost universally have what Richard Barnet called "well-developed power drives." They want to consolidate their position, increase their command. One effective ploy is to proclaim the existence of an enemy *out there. Forget our differences. We have to close ranks and pull together to defend ourselves. Stay the course. Follow me.* Internal problems recede, supplanted by the urgency of protection from dangers outside.

In this light we can understand the advice Secretary of State William Henry Seward gave to President Abraham Lincoln shortly before the outbreak of the Civil War. He suggested that rising unrest at home could be sidetracked by a vigorous foreign policy that included declaring war on Spain or France.

A century later, in Argentina, the generals actually tried it. The military junta which ruled the country and ruthlessly killed 20,000 of its own citizens was on the verge of collapse because of spreading street demonstrations and nationwide strikes. But when Argentina invaded the Falkland Islands in 1982, the demonstrations and strikes stopped instantly, and the country came together in an outpouring of nationalist fervor. Argentine unity was saved for the moment—until the British fleet regained control of the islands. Patriotic unity was quickly forgotten, unrest resumed, and the junta was ousted.

Manufactured Enemies

Sometimes a threat is readily plausible, as Germany in the Second World War. Sometimes it has to be created. The possibility of manufacturing enemies through the dynamics of projection is always present. In Jung's words, "It is in the nature of political bodies always to see the evil in the opposite group, just as the individual has an ineradicable tendency to get rid of everything he [or she] does not want to know about himself [or herself] by foisting it off on somebody else." The newly-created threat might be masked in the rhetoric of protecting national security or in pious platitudes of bringing democracy to benighted peoples.

The desire for supremacy on the part of one well-armed country easily leads to believing that another well-armed country desires supremacy for itself. For nearly half a century the United States and its capitalist allies assumed that the Soviet Union and its communist allies had the desire to dominate the world. It was a mirror image of the very same assumption the Soviet Union had of the West. The result was a long Cold War, which occasionally turned hot in places like Korea and Vietnam.

Whatever the outside threat, "our" people need to be protected against "them"—even if it is unclear who "they" are or why they're acting the way they are. Centuries ago William Hazlitt said that Daniel Defoe said, about his English compatriots, that there were a hundred thousand stout countryfellows ready to fight to the death against popery, "without knowing whether popery was a man or a horse." Label a group "terrorists," and many are willing to fight to the death against them, without knowing who they are or why they're ready to commit acts labeled terrorist.

Follow Me

In a haunting scene in the short Polish film *The Magician*, a man in a vaguely military uniform attracts a half-dozen boys to line up with toy popguns. He marches them to a carnival booth where pretty dolls are arrayed on shelves and orders them to shoot. When the boys are reluctant, the word "enemy" flashed on the screen over the dolls. The word has a magical effect. The boys draw themselves up, aim their guns, and smash the dolls.

The other side of the power drive is the assent of those who follow. It's true that respect for established authority is necessary for the smooth functioning of any society. Social education stresses its importance. Most members normally live within this framework when they know it's for the common good. But the same social constraints are often followed when the outcome is not good. Taking orders may relieve people of the anxiety of making their own decisions and accepting the consequences of their own initiatives, as well as alleviate distress over defying those in power. An emotional need may override a moral sense and lead people to accept leaders' dictates, whether right or wrong. "I was only following orders" is a standard excuse. And if those orders involve mistreating prisoners or blowing up families, they go through with it because it's someone else's responsibility, not theirs. And it is not just those with what are called authoritarian personalities (those who are happy to take orders and follow strong leaders) who do this; normally good, independent people also do this.

Tell It Like It Is

Winston Churchill called lies by public officials "terminological inexactitude." A nonviolent person is concerned with cutting through that inexactitude, identifying brutality and exploitation for what they are, bringing them out in the open so they can be dealt with.

The Nazis deliberately developed what they called "language rules" to make their anti-Semitic cruelty less repugnant. They spoke of "relocating" to "labor camps" rather than forced deportation to concentration camps. They talked about the "final solution" rather than mass murders in gas chambers. A security officer might speak of "intensive interrogation" when what's really going on is torture. The CIA's phrase "terminating with extreme prejudice" referred to assassination of enemy agents. In military language "softening up" enemy positions means unleashing massive bombing. "Collateral damage" refers to civilians who are killed.

A host of euphemisms tried to cover up what was really happening in the war against Iraq. Killing civilians was termed "degrading their resources." Unexploded cluster bombs that looked like toys but blew off the hands of Iraqi children were "stray ordinance." When U.S. soldiers engaged in looting, they were "helping themselves to souvenirs." And if they had to "drop a few civilians" who were in their way, well, that's war, they were "fighting for democracy."

Government employees who tried to give an acceptable face to the war had the title "Perception Managers." If they worked for an enemy country they would be called propagandists. The White House frequently referred to the nations that sent troops to Iraq a "coalition of the willing." Arundhati Roy described it as a "coalition of the bullied and bought." When the war was labeled "Operation Iraqi Freedom," she responded, "Empire is on the move, and Democracy is its sly new war cry."

Nonviolent criticism is aware of these language tricks and seeks to unmask them. It speaks straightforwardly to expose the atrocities and not let them be covered over with deliberately inoffensive terminology in the service of the group narcissism of nationalism.

Patriotism

Many modern nations are fragile coalitions of different ethnic, religious, and cultural groups, united under a shared flag and an idealized history, giving meaning and comfort to millions. Vatican II defined patriotism not as national pride, but in the context of the community of nations. "Citizens must cultivate a generous and loyal spirit of patriotism, but without being narrow-minded. This means that they will always direct their attention to the good of the whole human family, united by the different ties which bind together races, people and nations."[1]

"*Dulce et decorum est pro patria mori,*" Wilfred Owen wrote satirically during the First World War: "It is beautiful and proper to die for one's country." Every nation honors its citizens who die in battle. But, as George C. Scott's title character in the movie *Patton* put it more accurately, "The object of war is not to die for your country but to make the other bastard die for his." But this is not patriotism. Criticizing one's country when it destroys other members of the human family, when it acts arrogantly and without regard for international ties, fragile as they are, is a duty. And it is very patriotic.

Chapter 18

The Role of Anger

Theologian Edward Schillebeeckx has said that the peace of Christ in our time consists "in an inward discontent, in a prophetic protest against the situation as it is, and which is precisely not right the way it is." A person trying to be nonviolent can't help feeling deeply upset, inwardly discontent. In a world of warring nations, where so much injustice prevails at home and abroad, reactions of anger and grief at unilateral and unprovoked war, prison tortures, and blatant upward transfers of wealth are natural and healthy. It helps to know these reactions are a form of the peace of Christ.

I was taught as a child that anger is a "bad" emotion, one of the seven capital sins. We need to be clear about this. Anger is a normal human reaction to frustration, or a spontaneous sense of indignation when something strikes us as blatantly wrong. In trying to be more nonviolent we have to be able to separate destructive anger from constructive inward discontent.

I can now accept that some of my anger is justified. There really are people out there abusing children; there really are people out there deliberately starting wars; there really are people out there discriminating against and hurting others on the basis of race, religion, and a host of other factors; there really are people out there engaging in torture. I should feel anger about all of these. We need to nurse our feeling of outrage when a child is beaten, unarmed protesters are clubbed, prisoners are brutalized, families are massacred, the social safety net is dismantled, schools lack funding, people are denied health care.

Gandhi's nonviolence began with an experience of anger. The turning point in his life was a train incident in South Africa, when he was a young lawyer. He had purchased a first-class ticket for an overnight trip from Durban to Pretoria. In the middle of the night, a passenger complained about the presence of this "colored" man on the train. When Gandhi refused to go into a second-class compartment, he was unceremoniously thrown off the train at the next stop, Maritzburg, his luggage following close behind. On "that frigid night at Maritzburg," wrote one of his first biographers, Louis Fischer, "the germ of social protest was born in Gandhi." It stayed with him for a lifetime.

Martin Luther King Jr.'s protest energy also began with an experience of anger. He was fourteen years old, returning to Atlanta on a bus with his teacher after winning an oratorical contest. He described it later: "At a small town along the way, some white passengers boarded the bus, and the white driver ordered us to get up and give the whites our seats. We didn't move quickly enough to suit him, so he began cursing us, calling us 'black sons of bitches.' I intended to stay right in that seat, but Mrs. Bradley finally urged me up, saying we had to obey the law. And so we stood up in the aisle for the ninety miles to Atlanta. That night will never leave my memory. It was the angriest I have ever been in my life."[1]

New Testament Anger

Jesus got angry when he came across abuses. He was clearly angry when he drove the money changers out of the Temple. "Get these out of here! How dare you turn my Parent's home into a market!" (John 2:16) Another time he became very upset at some Pharisees: "He looked around at them in anger...deeply distressed at their stubborn hearts" (Mark 3:5a).

Paul was often filled with inward discontent when he came across something he considered an abuse. In Athens "he was greatly distressed to see the city full of idols" (Acts of the Apostles 17:16). The original Greek word, *paraxuno*, can also mean "stirred," "provoked," "exasperated." Paul was greatly distressed, provoked, disturbed, upset—angry—at the idolatrous ambience of Athens, as we today might be disturbed or upset—angry—at the bullying abuses of the powerful against the powerless.

An Example: Torture

According to former CIA agent John Stockwell, U.S. advisors in the 1970s trained Uruguayan security forces in torture techniques. They first taught the theory of torture: what kinds of electrical shocks to use, what parts of the body were most sensitive, how to inflict pain and keep the victim conscious, how far to go before the victim dies. Then they had the police go out into Montevideo late at night and pick up men and women who were on the streets or sleeping in parks. These homeless people were brought to the torture laboratories and used as subjects on which to practice the techniques learned in the classroom. They were tortured until they died. Afterwards their bodies were thrown back on the streets where they served as a warning to the citizens of Uruguay to beware of the security police—and their U.S. advisors.

When I first heard this I felt very angry. Torture itself is bad enough, and, as far as I'm concerned, always inexcusable and unjustifiable. But here was torture to the death of the poorest of the poor—for the sake of learning how to torture better. I was angry at those who could perpetrate such cold-blooded inhumanity. I was also angry at my country whose policies in Latin America led to atrocities like this.

During the war against Iraq, the U.S. Defense Department sought legal advice about how far interrogators could go in questioning captives. When the legal advice became known to the public, it was clear that permitted interrogation techniques could involve inflicting pain, humiliation, beatings, death threats, deprivation of food and water—and it wouldn't be called torture.

This gave legal justification to the torture by U.S. military personnel of Iraqi prisoners in 2004, which contributed to an unsurprising outburst of anger there. One Iraqi put it, "This kind of humiliation must lead to revenge." In fact it aggravated the prolonged attacks against U.S. forces and their allies, including the torture of beheading.

Anger's Energy

Without the energy of anger we can easily become lethargic

about the un-rightness of the world and situations such as torture. Unless directly affected by injustice, we can read about the troubles described in the morning paper, shrug them off: "There's nothing I can do about it." We can take "the poor you will always have with you" (Matt. 26:11) as a literal prophecy and sigh with resignation. For some, it may be easy to turn away and stop caring, salve our consciences with many little tasks, or try to forget it all with television or our drug of choice, to lapse into Sartrean bad faith.

But if we are energized by anger we want to act. We resonate deep down to the French revolutionaries' cry, *Ecrasez l'infame*, crush the infamous thing, eliminate the cause of the trouble. Anger is energizing. When we see something is wrong (or experience the wrongdoing) and are angry, we generate the energy to do something about it, as Gandhi did, as King did. Anger is a powerful motivator for action. We know that the world doesn't have to be in the mess it's in. Human beings have made certain decisions—to go to war, for instance, or to engage in ethnic cleansing or not to provide funding for human needs—and human beings can change those decisions. Our anger impels us to work to change them, but change them through active nonviolence, converting, not hurting.

We recognize the trembling feeling of outrage associated with this true patriotism, outrage directed against those responsible for unilateral wars, responsible for atrocities, responsible for the violation of the community of nations. Our challenge is to transmute that feeling into a determination to bring about constructive change in a nonviolent way. What makes us violent or nonviolent is not the anger we feel, but what we do with our anger.

Part Seven

Jesus and the Empire

The winds of empire blowing today are troublesome to anyone who would be personally nonviolent. A spirituality grounded in the nonviolent Christ pays careful attention to Jesus' attitude toward the dominant empire of his day, how he and his earliest followers reacted to and were affected by it, and their strong convictions, expressed in the book of Revelation, that empire was ultimately doomed.

Chapter 19

Rome and the Messiah

The controversial 2004 film *The Passion of the Christ* down-played the role of the Roman empire in Jesus' suffering and death. It played up the participation of the Jewish priestly officials. Although they were the ones most sensitive to his messianic impli-cations and the ones who turned him in on the charge of sedition, Jesus' passion was inflicted during Roman occupation, by Roman authorities, under the Roman imperial imperative. His death was sentenced by the Roman governor and carried out by Roman sol-diers.

In New Testament times the Roman empire was the overrid-ing political force in southern and eastern Europe, northern Africa, and the Middle East. That awesome entity comprised the largest amount of disparate territory for a longer time than any other empire in history. Some have possessed more land, like the British, but not for anywhere near the four-hundred-year duration of the Romans. The present U.S. empire, although the most powerful in history so far, has yet to prove it has Roman-caliber staying power.

Imperial Rome had ruled Jesus' homeland for over half a cen-tury before his birth. Roman soldiers were garrisoned in strategic locations throughout his homeland, ready to put down any stir-rings of discontent. Jesus' people were kept in check by the armed might of the Roman legions. Their ancestors, who considered themselves specially chosen by God and had fought for freedom against Philistines, Egyptians, Assyrians, Babylonians, and Greeks, now were reluctantly chafing under this new conqueror.

Pax Romana operated on the principle of peace through strength. Roman violence was never far beneath the surface in the Holy Land of Jesus' day. They tortured to death rebels they cap-tured. They forced people at swordpoint to carry military equipment. They garrisoned soldiers at conspicuous sites: in Capernaum by the lake, in Sepphoris near Nazareth, in Jerusalem close to the Temple, in Caesarea, their headquarters on the coast.

Imperial Hubris

Empire, then as now, exists primarily for power and profit. Those who control it might make lofty claims of establishing law and order, or bringing a higher civilization, or establishing the true religion. But the principal payoffs are enrichment at the expense of subservient populations and the satisfaction of dominating others.

The Romans had an overwhelming sense of superiority. They were proud of their generosity in allowing inferior people to participate in their great enterprise. If asked why they were in Spain or Africa or Greece—or Palestine—they would have answered that they offered their subjects something far better than independence: the opportunity of sharing in the magnificence of the Empire itself.

Rome had taken control of what they called Palestine in 63 BCE. What they wanted there was territory and taxes. They needed the territory to control that small but strategic strip of land which for centuries had been the passageway between Africa and Asia. They also wanted money. The Roman denarius, with its image of Caesar on one side, was the coin of exchange in the Palestine of Jesus' day. Taxes had to be paid to that Caesar.

The Romans farmed out tax collection to commercial companies which in turn employed a large number of strong-armed men called publicans. Their job was to come up with the money by any means necessary. If they collected more than their quota they could keep the surplus, no questions asked. Provinces of the empire were expected to collect enough to pay for their own administration and to insure a constant flow of money to Rome.

The process was backed up by the fearsome Roman legions. A few of these troops were born in Italy, but most came from the conquered tribes of Europe, Africa, or the Middle East. If they were not already Roman citizens, they were given this honor when they signed on for their near-lifetime terms of thirty years of active duty followed by five more in the reserves. Few of those who were stationed in Palestine could speak Aramaic, the language of Jesus' homeland.

As citizens with an active interest in the empire, these legionnaires had a tangible stake in its power and property. They tended to regard the empire's enemies as outlaws and criminals and treated them with predictable harshness.

Collaborators

The Roman governor of Palestine, as any good imperial overseer, allowed the local political and religious establishment to direct the day-to-day lives of the people. The highest Jewish authority was the Sanhedrin, a council of seventy-one members, many of them from the wealthy, aristocratic Sadducees party. The high priest of the year was its convener and president. It had jurisdiction over all religious and legal matters, except for offenses against Rome (understood as anything that constituted a threat to imperial rule).

To say that these religious and political leaders were collaborators is both realistic and understandable. The word has an unpleasant ring. But given Roman imperial might, the alternative to going along with the Romans was to risk imprisonment and even death.

Most people in Judea, Samaria, and Galilee went about their business, ignoring the Roman presence as much as they could. Like occupied people everywhere, they tried to avoid being squeezed too tightly by their conquerors. Many came to terms with these foreigners in the way conquered people have done throughout history: don't bother them and they won't bother you.

Rebellion

But revolution was in the air. When the Zealots, a group of daring men under the leadership of Judas of Galilee, raided an arms supply depot in Sepphoris, the Romans rounded up two thousand suspected revolutionaries and crucified them along the road to Nazareth, six miles away. This happened in the year 6 CE. Jesus would have been about ten years old. He may well have seen the crosses.

These Zealots were similar in ideology to the Pharisees, strict observers of the Mosaic Law, who had separated themselves from the mainstream of society and, because of their zeal to see the Law practiced without outside interference, refused to obey the Romans. Zealots were not willing to wait patiently for a future Messiah. They wanted to become actively involved in the messianic transformation of their people by driving out the Romans. In their fundamentalist beliefs and their revolutionary zeal they were similar to the Taliban and to the followers of Osama bin Laden.

Zealots established hiding places in the nearly-inaccessible eastern slopes of the hill country of Judea. From there they could make lightning-quick strikes on the occupying forces. The Romans looked on them as robbers and bandits. The Sanhedrin considered them dangerous disturbers of the peace. In the eyes of most of the people, they were heroes.

At least one of Jesus' closest disciples, Simon, was a Zealot. Another, Judas Iscariot, may well have been. The origin of his name is obscure. It could well have been derived from the Latin *siccarius*, dagger-man, a word the Romans used for an armed revolutionary.

The Subversive One

The Gospels do not portray Jesus as a Zealot, eager for an armed uprising to overthrow the Roman occupation. The revolutionary character of his life lay in the ideas he promulgated and in his personal stance toward the society of his time, including the empire. His main theme, according to the Synoptic Gospels, was that the Reign of God was at hand. Mark summarized it: "Jesus went into Galilee, proclaiming the good news of God. 'The time has come,' he said. 'The kindom of God is near. Repent and believe the good news'" (Mark 1:14-15).

The kindom of God was a familiar image to his listeners. It was to be a realm of peace, where the lion would lie down with the lamb, and all nations would worship the true God. They, the chosen people, would receive choice blessings. (See, for instance, Isaiah 65:17-25.) The hated Romans would no longer be a problem.

This great earthly panorama, in which the splendors of heaven would be mirrored in the joy and blessedness of all creation in final harmony, would be brought about, they believed, through the instrumentality of a special envoy sent by God—an anointed one, the Messiah. Many thought that Jesus, because of his teachings and miracles, was this Messiah. His dramatic entrance into Jerusalem on Palm Sunday was accompanied by an enthusiastic crowd acclaiming him in messianic terms.

Jesus had indeed preached that the messianic kindom was near. But none of its expected characteristics were in evidence. When John the Baptist sent his followers to inquire if Jesus was the expected Messiah, Jesus evaded a direct answer. Instead, he indicated that what was happening was quite different from what most people thought the kindom would look like. "Go back and report to John what you hear and see: the blind receive sight, the lame walk, those who have leprosy are cured, the deaf hear, the dead are raised, and the good news is preached to the poor" (Matthew 11:4-5).

He was describing an entirely different set-up than his co-religionists expected. If Jesus' teaching ran counter to the prevailing climate of opinion, so did his actions. He was a friend of outcasts, criminals, prostitutes, and, above all, the poor, with whom he spent most of his time. He did not have a steady job, did not settle down, get married, and raise a family. He repudiated wealth and consistently refused to provide for his own security. He differed significantly from the prevailing attitudes about what constituted a normal life. But it got right to the heart of what the kindom of heaven as he saw it was all about.

It was a completely different society from that of the Roman overlords. The kindom Jesus preached has been the stuff of revolutionary ideals over the centuries—replace the existing order based on power and profit with a new order based on compassion and caring. But, according to Jesus, this was not to be done through violent overthrow and killing the oppressors, rather through personal witness and conversion of heart.

Today we would call it active nonviolence.

Chapter 20

The Imperial Hammer

One doubts that the Roman governor and his staff knew much about this. Roman intelligence had not identified Jesus as dangerous. But the collaborators knew and were threatened by him. In the new society Jesus pictured, everyone would be fundamentally equal. No one would be pushed aside because of poverty or sickness or old age. Sharing and caring would be the outstanding features. If this new community developed, the structures of the old society would crumble. They could see clearly that, if large numbers of people began to live in the way he was calling for, the Sanhedrin's positions of prominence would decline precipitously.

Jesus was threatening their power and place in a more decisive way than the Roman overlords, with whom they had reached an accommodation. He was even more dangerous than the armed rebels in the hills. In the unlikely event that the Zealots were successful and the Romans driven out, religious structures of the society would have continued. But if Jesus' way came to prevail, that structure would be thoroughly undermined.

Jesus was doing what no political leaders can long tolerate. He was infecting the people with ideas that ran contrary to the patterns that continued the power of those in leadership. If enough people no longer believe in or will tolerate those patterns, the whole thing begins to fall apart. If the danger was not apparent in rural Galilee, it was clear in urban Jerusalem. Jesus had to be stopped. As they saw it, he was a danger to the nation.

Get Him

Jesus was perceived as inciting unrest, creating a climate of resistance to established authority. If it went much further, the immediate danger was that the Romans would hear about it and not tolerate it. Roman patience with disturbances like this could be easily exhausted. The fearsome legions could quickly and indiscriminately crush the Jewish society. The Sanhedrin wanted to avoid that catastrophe.

The decision to have Jesus eliminated was taken in a national security context. The gospel of John described it.

> Then the chief priests and the Pharisees called a meeting of the Sanhedrin. "What are we accomplishing?" they asked. "Here is this man performing many miraculous signs. If we let him go on like this, everyone will believe in him, and then the Romans will come and take away both our place and our nation." Then one of them, named Caiaphas, who was high priest that year, spoke up, "You know nothing at all! You do not realize that it is better for you that one man die for the people than that the whole nation perish."...So from that day on they plotted to take his life (John 11:47-50, 53).

The Sanhedrin had to present Jesus to the Roman authorities in such a way that they would judge him guilty of death. This was not hard to do. The Romans were notoriously quick against anyone suspected of insurrection. And that was precisely the charge under which the Sanhedrin brought Jesus to the Romans—sedition. "And they began to accuse him, saying, 'We have found this man subverting our nation. He opposes payment of taxes to Caesar and claims to be Christ, a king...He stirs up the people all over Judea by his teaching. He started in Galilee and has come all the way here'" (Luke 23:2,5).

Jesus was presented to the Roman authorities as a revolutionary. The Sanhedrin was on the side of the Romans. In the sycophantic words of the collaborators, "We have no king but Caesar" (John 19:15b).

The Messiah and the Governor

The Roman investigation of the charges against Jesus would be cursory, at best. The Governor of Judea, Pontius Pilate, would conduct it himself.

Pilate, like many provincial governors, was a procurator, someone with prior experience in Roman financial affairs. Few of these procurator-governors were honest, history tells us. Most were interested in money not only for the Empire, but also for themselves. During their tour of duty they followed the unwritten custom to accumulate as much as the traffic would bear.

Pilate was a bureaucrat on the make in Rome's foreign service. He had been assigned to the tiny but troublesome territory of Palestine rather than to a more promising post in Egypt or Dalmatia. The Jewish historian Philo reported that Pilate's rule in Judea was marked by "corruption, violence, depredations, ill-treatments, offenses, numerous illegal executions, and incessant, unbearable cruelty." Pilate was not a nice man.

He had dismayed pious Jews when he confiscated Temple funds to build an aqueduct. He offended their sensitivity to idolatry by ordering to Jerusalem soldiers carrying banners decorated with images of the emperor. He held the power of life and death over everyone in Palestine.

But Jesus rejected Pilate's authority. He was not at all impressed with the implements of Roman rule. Pilate had power— the steel of the legions—but he did not have legitimacy. Pilate, and the imperial power he represented, had no right to be in charge of Palestine. Their rule was based on conquest, on violence, on fear. Jesus refused to play Pilate's power game.

When Pilate brought him in for face-to-face questioning, Jesus showed him no special deference. Pilate: "Don't you realize I have power either to free you or to crucify you?" Jesus: "You would have no power over me if it were not given to you from above" (John 19:10-11). Nor did he try to defend himself. "Pilate asked him, 'Aren't you going to answer? See how many things they are accusing you of.' But Jesus still made no reply" (Mark 15:4).

Jesus might have tried to ingratiate himself, picking up on Pilate's attempt to start a philosophical conversation about the nature of truth. He might have pursued the governor's initial reluctance to convict. "Then Pilate said to chief priests and to the people, 'I find no basis for a charge against this man'" (Luke 23:4). He might have tried to win Pilate over by explaining away the accusations against him to the governor's satisfaction.

Even had he engaged in dialogue and secured Pilate's approval, he would have lost it a few minutes later when Pilate succumbed to career ambition under pressure by the priests. "If you let this man go, you are no friend of Caesar. Anyone who claims to be a king opposes Caesar," the collaborators clamored (John 19:12).

That did it. Whatever residue of resistance Pilate possessed evaporated in the harsh reality of imperial politics. The pragmatic Pilate pulled himself together. Threatened with accusations of disloyalty, he gave in, made the messy decision of a mediocre bureaucrat muddling through, and sentenced Jesus to death—just another rebel suspect. He ordered the accused rebel Jesus to be crucified, along with two others whom Matthew's gospel (*New American Bible* translation) clearly calls "revolutionaries" (Matthew 27:38).

The Professional Killers

"Finally Pilate handed him over to them to be crucified. So the soldiers took charge of Jesus" (John 19:16). The Roman execution squad took over. It was nothing personal; executioners seldom are. They had nothing against him as an individual. Their specialty was efficient crucifixion. Hurt the prisoner enough to suffer, but not enough to faint. Fasten him to the cross, with spikes if necessary, then hoist him up in a public place where everyone could see his agony, where his torturous death would serve as a deterrent. Stay around until he died, to make sure nobody interfered. They didn't have to wait long for Jesus, only a few hours. As a bonus, the execution squad got to keep any personal belongings the victim carried. Jesus had only what he was wearing. "They divided up his clothes by casting lots" (Matthew 27:35).

The execution of Jesus, the Galilean teacher who had antagonized some highly placed Jews, was a minor moment for the

Romans. An unexceptional governor had ordered the anticipated death of someone who had caused a minor nuisance to the Empire. The whole affair from the Roman side was an example of what Hannah Arendt called "the banality of evil."

Smash

The dreaded Roman crunch, which the chief priests and the Pharisees of the Sanhedrin had feared, was deferred. But not for long. It came in the year 70, when four Roman legions, twenty thousand hardened troops under a general named Titus, crushed an outbreak of violence, captured Jerusalem, and burned down the Temple. Three years later, when the last fortress of Masada on the Dead Sea was overcome and its defenders committed suicide, all resistance ended.

The conquerors carried the seven-branched candlestick from the Temple back to Rome in triumph, an event carved in stone on the memorial erected there to Titus. The image on the arch can be seen in Rome today.

The ancient nation of Israel, whose security its leaders had been so concerned to preserve, was destroyed and its people scattered.

The New Beginning

But the ideas and expectations Jesus had taught survived. And they spread more widely and more rapidly, through the power of his resurrection, than anyone dared hope before his death. The overall imperative of his teaching was clear. Even under the yoke of empire, not only is it wrong to kill, it is even wrong to hate an enemy. War-makers are not blessed, peacemakers are.

Jesus' earliest followers showed that they had gotten the message. Within a few weeks after his death, inspired by their experience with the risen Jesus, they went about doing the same kinds of things he had done, carrying on his work.

As their Teacher had run into opposition, so did they. He had given them notice. "Do not suppose that I have come to bring peace on the earth. I did not come to bring peace, but a sword" (Matthew 10:34). Luke's version of these words (12:51) tell us that the metaphorical sword meant "division." The disciples' healing and preaching brought about considerable division, the same kind of division Jesus had brought about—and gave them the same opportunity to exercise courage in the face of the enemies they soon had to face.

Those whose power was threatened responded in the way of power. They tried to put these new preachers and healers out of circulation. The disciples frequently found themselves in prison. They were thrown in jail so often that, as William Stringfellow suggested, the Acts of the Apostles might more appropriately be entitled the Arrests of the Apostles.

Arrests, and more. One of the early believers, Stephen, was brutally beaten to death, stoned, as described in Acts 7:57-60. When Paul was arrested yet again in his stormy career, the Roman commander of the area ordered that he undergo intensive interrogation. "He directed that he be flogged and questioned in order to find out why the people were shouting at him like this" (Acts 22:24). The Acts of the Apostles stops abruptly with Paul under house arrest in Rome for two years awaiting trial.

Before the century ended, many followers of Jesus' way had endured persecution and death at the hands of the same murderous empire which had crucified Jesus. Somehow, they were confident, justice would be brought about, the Kindom of God would be established.

Chapter 21

The Verdict

As Jesus' movement spread throughout other provinces, the empire would take similar repressive actions against his followers. Before the end of the first century, one of them, who used the name John, would employ the literary apocalyptic genre then in vogue, filled with extravagant symbolism and astounding visions, to pen in graphic detail a scathing indictment of that empire. It would be a prophetic verdict on Empire's works and pomp. It would also serve as the climatic conclusion of what became the New Testament.

The book of the Revelation of John has been subject to many interpretations. But fundamentally it's about Empire—and the people of faith who live in empires. It's about the dominant empire at the time the book was written, and by extension about any empire that exerts the same callous control over subjects near and far.

Using imagery only thinly veiled, Revelation's author described Rome as the new Babylon, the new power threatening God's people as ancient Babylon had threatened earlier generations. It's the great prostitute sitting on "seven hills" (17:9), "drunk with the blood of the saints, the blood of those who bore testimony to Jesus" (17:6). To make sure his readers got the point that it's about Rome, the author added, "The woman you saw is the great city that rules over the kings of the earth" (17:18).

The Satanic Dragon

Revelation's imagery brought to center stage the transterrestrial adversary of the people of God. "Another sign appeared in the sky, it was a huge red dragon, with seven heads and ten horns"

(12:3). This dragon, red like spilled blood, had seven (the number of completeness) crowned heads, indicating the fullness of its control over the whole world. Its horns symbolized its power—ten of them, the number of multitude. Its power was immense. And the dragon was now here, in the world. "War broke out in heaven: Michael and his angels battled against the dragon…The huge dragon, the ancient serpent, who is called the Devil and Satan, who deceived the whole world, was thrown down to earth" (12:7, 9). The dragon, having lost the battle of Heaven, is relegated to the realm of humans, there to wreak havoc.

Satan, pictured as a bloody and strong dragon, is the power behind the Empire, which is portrayed as a second frightful beast coming "out of the sea with ten horns and seven heads" (13:1). "To it the dragon gave its own power and throne, along with great authority" (13:2b). Fascinated, "the whole world followed after the beast" (13:3b).

"Who can compare with the beast or who can fight against it?" Revelation (13:4b) asked. From the perspective of those early followers of Jesus, the evil empire appeared invincible. No one, it seemed, could contest it.

"The beast…was given authority to act for forty-two months" (13:5). These forty-two months are not literal. They mean three and a half years (half of seven, the number of completeness). They symbolically designate the mainstream of history, the middle of the flow, when Revelation's readers were living. During this tremulous time, somewhere between Creation and End, the beast, Rome, was "allowed to wage war against the holy ones and conquer them, and it was granted authority over every tribe, people, tongue, and nation" (13:7).

This is the way it must have seemed to those followers of Jesus, those "holy ones" under threat from the empire, which Revelation portrays as a beast in the service of Satan.

The Antichrist

There's more to come. After the Satanic dragon and the imperial beast, yet another ugly image emerged. "Then I saw another beast come up out of the earth; it had two horns like a lamb's but spoke like a dragon" (13:11). The insidious Antichrist. It looks tender as a lamb, but its mission is straight from the devil. Did the author of Revelation intend some definite individual person here? Perhaps, but the images keep shifting. "It [the antichrist] was then permitted to breathe life into the beast's image, so that the beast's image could speak and could have anyone who did not worship it put to death" (13:15). Those who were bringing the imperial beast into the homes of Christians were agents of the Empire who reinforced the decree: worship or be punished. They would be the police, the army, the judges, the jailers, the executioners—collectively the antichrist.

This antichrist beast "forced all the people, small and great, rich and poor, free and slave, to be given a stamped image on their right hands or their foreheads, so that no one could buy or sell except one who had the stamped image of the beast's name or the number that stood for its name" (13:16-17). The stamped image would be familiar to readers at the time as a sign of slavery. Slaves were branded with a symbol of their owners. It is as though Christians were being treated as slaves of the Empire, forced to do its bidding, unable to worship freely, unable even to buy or sell anything without the Empire's approval. Revelation's view of life in the Empire is from down under, a portrayal that would be immediately grasped by anyone in jeopardy from the minions of the Empire.

Even the number of the Antichrist is further evidence of how early Christians saw agents of the Empire. "Wisdom is needed here; one who understands can calculate the number of the beast...six hundred and sixty six" (13:18). Wisdom is needed, all right, wisdom to understand the symbolism of the numbers. Seven signifies fullness or completion. Six would be short of perfection but deceptively so. If one looked at a pile of something quickly, it would be hard at a glance to distinguish seven of them from six. It's deceptive. And three is a number of perfection. Three sevens would be complete perfection. Three sixes would be deceptive imperfection. The beast-Empire and its beast-agents, then, seem awesome, but their 666 identifies them as perfectly imperfect.

And it's all going to come crashing down. Revelation presents visions of massive uprisings. The people conquered by the Empire, those kings seduced by it, will turn on it. They "will hate the harlot [Rome]; they will leave her desolate and naked; they will eat her flesh and consume her with fire" (17:16). "Pay her back as she has paid others. Pay her back double for her deeds...To the measure of her boasting and wantonness repay her in torment and grief" (18:6-7b).

Popping in and out of the book is this intuitive sense of how the Roman Empire will come to an end: the conquered nations will turn on it from outside, and internal corruption and rebellion will do it in from the inside. "With such force will Babylon the great city be thrown down, and will never be found again" (18:21b).

Armageddon

Now comes the climatic clash, mixing heaven and earth, the symbolic battle of Armageddon. It featured the beast that was Rome along with its puppets, "the kings of the earth and their armies" (19:18) against "the armies of heaven" (19:14). The leader of the heavenly hosts "wore a cloak that had been dipped in blood, and his name was called the Word of God" (19:13). Here's Jesus, the conquering hero, at the head of the celestial militia.

The battle of Armageddon recapitulates the downfall of the Empire, with the armies of heaven as the agents of the downfall. Revelation is discrete here. We're not to be titillated by scenes of carnage. We're only given Armageddon's outcome—glorious victory by the heavenly hosts and utter defeat of the Empire. "The beast [the empire] was caught and with it the false prophet [its agents] who had performed in its sight the signs by which he led astray those who had accepted the mark of the beast and those who had worshipped its image. The two were thrown alive into the fiery pool burning with sulfur" (19:20).

Quietly, prosaically, almost coldly, the text simply states, "The rest were killed by the sword that came out of the mouth of the one riding the horse" (19:21), the warrior Jesus. We're left with only one gory detail at the end of the verse: "and all the birds gorged themselves on their flesh." Vultures voraciously devoured the carrion. Take THAT, you evil empire. The magnificent Roman imperial world will be reduced to vulture food.

The Divine Zap

But it's not the ultimate defeat of the ultimate adversary, the supreme power of evil, not just yet. "When the thousand years are completed, Satan will be released from his prison. He will go out to deceive the nations at the four corners of the earth, Gog and Magog, to gather them for battle; their number is like the sand of the sea" (20:7-8).

This scene is so anti-climactic that it fails to generate the juices that Armageddon did. The really intrusive trouble, the Roman Empire, is already done away with. But Revelation needs to tie up the remaining loose end, the source of the Empire's evil, Satan. The writer hurriedly summarizes the gathering of more enemies, symbolized by names from chapter 38 of the prophecy of Ezekiel, Gog and Magog.

As though the writer knows we're failing to feel any anticipation, failing in fact to feel much of anything now, Gog and Magog and everyone else are quickly disposed of with a stroke of the pen: "But fire came down from heaven and consumed them" (20:9b). That's it, gone in a burst of flame, the Divine Zap.

The author does put a little feeling into the verse that completes the scene. "The Devil who had led them astray was thrown into the pool of fire and sulphur, where the beast and the false prophet were. There they will be tormented day and night forever and ever" (20:10). The Devil won't just be defeated, won't be annihilated either. That wouldn't be good enough. The source of all evil must be tortured eternally, along with the beast—that's the Empire, Revelation reader—and the oily, ugly Antichrist, all thrown into the pool of burning sulphur, where they will be tormented day and night forever and ever. And ever, and ever, and ever, and ever. Forever is a long, long time.

This last part caters to an understandable Christian desire for revenge. Revelation's readers can feel a sense of satisfaction, vicarious revenge, in enjoying the description of their enemies getting their just due. The verdict is in, the sentence carried out. How sweet it is.

The Grand Finale
Revelation's last vision should be read with glorious, full orchestral music in the background.

> Then I saw new heavens and a new earth. The former heavens and the former earth had passed away, and the sea existed no longer. I also saw a new Jerusalem, the holy city, coming down out of heaven from God, beautiful as a bride and groom on their wedding day. And I heard a loud voice calling from the throne, "Look! God's tabernacle is among humanity! God will live with them; they will be God's people, and God will be fully present among them. The Most High will wipe away every tear from their eyes. And death, mourning, crying and pain will be no more, for the old order has fallen" (21:1-4).

The enemy is vanquished forever. The faithful now enjoy the fullness of life in a heavenly-earthly city, a transformed and glorious Jerusalem of biblical sanctity, where all is sweetness and light, where "death, mourning, crying and pain will be no more" (21:4), where beauty and serenity prevail.

The One on the throne says, in effect, this is it, this is the end, finally. Evoking the memory of Jesus' living water discourse, where he spoke of giving "a spring of water welling up to eternal life" (John 4:14), evoking also the primordial delight in Eden where a river watered the Garden (Genesis 2:10), the One on the throne says, "to the thirsty I will give a gift from the spring of life-giving water" (Revelation 21:6b).

Then, as an ever-present reminder to readers of Revelation, the One on the throne says, "But as for cowards, the unfaithful, the depraved, murderers, the unchaste, sorcerers, idol-worshipers, and deceivers of every sort, their lot is in the burning pool of fire

and sulfur, which is the second death" (21:8).
Don't become complacent, Revelation readers.
Although it specifically addressed the empire of its time, the book of Revelation gives a biblical verdict on Empire itself. Its judgment is that all empires are doomed if they maintain their imperial course. But we who confront empires in the spirit of the nonviolent Christ can transform their faces, confident in the help he promised: "I am with you always, until the end of the age" (Matthew 28:20).

Part Eight

A Nonviolent Vision

The Brazilian theologian, Leonardo Boff, has written, "Wherever an authentically human life is growing in the world, wherever justice is triumphing over the instincts of domination...wherever love is getting the better of selfish interest, and wherever hope is resisting the lure of cynicism or despair—there the process of resurrection is being turned into reality. It will continue to operate everywhere until the final transfiguration of the world is achieved in the definitive parousia of the Lord." [1]

Our efforts are never in vain. Everything we do nonviolently for someone, for justice in Iraq or down the block, for reconciliation at home or abroad, is making the world a better place, is helping bring about Jesus' Kindom.

Chapter 22

Sowing Nonviolent Seeds

Dorothy Day once said, "Our work is to sow. Another generation will be reaping the harvest." Johnny Appleseed also went about sowing seeds:

> The Lord's been good to me.
> And so I thank the Lord
> For giving me the things I need,
> The sun and the rain and the apple seed.
> The Lord's been good to me.

The legend of Johnny Appleseed, who wandered through the Midwest in the early 19th century sowing with generous abundance, was based on the life of a real person named John Chapman. As a boy in Massachusetts he had a habit of wandering away on long trips in search of birds and flowers. In 1801 his wandering took him down the Ohio River, paddling a strange craft of two canoes lashed together and filled with decaying apples he had brought from the cider presses of western Pennsylvania. John Chapman planted his first apple orchard two miles downriver from Steubenville, Ohio.

After returning to Pennsylvania for more seeds, he continued planting. Besides the apples for which he became famous, Chapman sowed seeds of many healing herbs. Indigenous peoples of the area considered him a great medicine man. Apple orchards grew and flourished in what had been the wilderness of Ohio and Indiana, thanks to the man who became forever known as Johnny Appleseed.

Biblical Sowing

Another seed-sowing image comes from the troubled terrain of Palestine, a world away from the fertile fields of Ohio. "Hear this! A sower went out to sow. And as he sowed, some seed fell on the path, and the birds came and ate it up. Other seed fell on rocky ground, where it had little soil. It sprang up at once, because the soil was not deep. And when the sun rose, it was scorched and it withered for lack of roots. Some seed fell among thorns, and the thorns grew up and choked it, and it produced no grain. And some seed fell on rich soil and produced fruit. It came up and grew and yielded thirty-, sixty-, and even a hundred-fold" (Mark 4:3-8).

When seed-sowing works, as it did in this parable, as it did for John Chapman, it's like magic. The seed multiplies thirty, sixty or even a hundred times. The wondrous power packed in the tiny seeds interacts with the nutrients in the soil to produce bushels of apples in Ohio or fields of grain in Galilee.

Power Seeds

Seeds of nonviolence are alive with power and energy. Sometimes they blow in with their hidden power from unexpected sources. A letter in the *New York Times* described some in a part of the world not known for its nonviolence:

> Once, in Damascus, when I was strolling along the street called Straight, I watched as a man who was riding slowly through the crowd on a bicycle with a basket of oranges precariously balanced on the handlebars was bumped by a porter so bent by a heavy burden that he had not seen him. The burden was dropped, the oranges scattered and a bitter altercation broke out between the two men, surrounded by a circle of onlookers. After an angry exchange of shouted insults, as the bicyclist moved toward the porter with a clenched fist, a tattered little man slipped from the crowd, took the raised fist in his hands and kissed it. A murmur of approval ran through the watchers, the antagonists relaxed, then the people began picking up the oranges and the little man drifted away.[1]

Another witness described a different scene from another part of the world:

> In Moscow, in what was then the Soviet Union, hundreds of people gathered outside the Parliament during the August 1991 attempted coup. They built barricades of trolley cars, buses, old pieces of metal and box springs— not so much because that would stop the tanks for more than a few minutes, but to enable them to enter into dialogue with the attacking soldiers. Mothers and girls gave the soldiers cakes, food, kisses and flowers, and asked them not to kill their mothers, sisters, and brothers. One friend brought roses and distributed them to the soldiers and gave them a hug, saying, "Don't shoot. Be kind to the people."[2]

Instead of anxious self-concern, nonviolent seeds contain compassionate other-concern, like that shown by the old man on the street named Straight in Damascus or the women outside the Parliament building in Moscow.

Rich Soil

Nonviolent seeds have power to change minds and hearts when the soil on which they fall is fertile. And it often is, much more often than we might imagine. "Nonviolence is the law of our species," Gandhi said, "as violence is the law of the brute." He considered it to be so congruent with our nature that he considered it a natural law. "I claim that even now, though the social structure is not based on a conscious acceptance of non-violence, all the world over [humanity] lives and...[people] retain their possessions on the sufferance of one another. If they had not done so, only the fewest and the most ferocious would have survived. But such is not the case. Families are bound together by ties of love, and so are groups in the so-called civilized society called nations."[3]

Gandhian nonviolence appeals to something deep in our

hearts. People really do hunger for decency, even those whose life experiences have made them hard and aggressive. The sower of nonviolent seed does not let a hard and aggressive exterior deter from extending a hand of friendship. When the seeds fall on the generous and creative side of human nature they find the fertile soil that, miracle-like, produces the many-fold grain.

And then we find—another miracle—that they multiply. When we give away material possessions, we have less of them. But intangible riches increase when they're shared. When we appreciate the gifts of nature, when we communicate compassion, when we sidestep an attack and respond with dialogue, we find that our nonviolent seeds don't run out. They increase, they multiply. We have more to give. And those who receive from us, when their ground is fertile, start multiplying still more.

Seeds for All Seasons

All of us can sow nonviolent seeds in the everyday world in which we live and move and have our being. Even if we can't solve the intractable violence of the Middle East, or end genocide in Africa, every one of our personal interactions can be engaged in with a greater degree of sensitivity, with a conscious effort to avoid words or deeds that hurt and an equally conscious effort to say and do what will help.

"In the end, it is the reality of personal relationships that saves everything," Thomas Merton wrote. We can meet nonviolently the challenges of discord and violence in our lives. We can model nonviolent conflict resolution and engage in community building. We can expose suffering in distant parts of the world or across town. We can protest pre-emptive wars. The possibilities are limitless. The fields are vast; the seeds are potent. And the results can be awe-inspiring.

Chapter 23

Persevering Witness

The important thing is that we do something, not everything. And that we stay with it, continue the course, hang in there. Our engagement could be at home or in the neighborhood, about family problems or community unrest. It could be broader—civil rights, women's rights, gay rights, abolition of capital punishment, prison reform. It could be international—energy alternatives, weapons control, nuclear disarmament.

For years, a spotlight of national attention has been brought to bear on Fort Benning in Georgia, home of what had been innocuously called the School of the Americas. This "school" is in fact a training ground for Latin American military officers in techniques of internal repression. Over 60,000 military personnel have been taught not only the latest combat skills, but also psychological warfare, including torture. Under pressure from the protests that drew thousands of peace activists to the base each November, the Pentagon changed the institution's name to the Western Hemisphere Institute for Security Cooperation. Its mission remained the same. The protests continued.

No one can do everything, but it's important to do something. After the first U.S. war against Iraq in the early 1990s, a woman from Chicago, Kathy Kelly, began Voices in the Wilderness (VITW). Its purpose was to cry out about the suffering of the Iraqi people in the aftermath of the war. They organized groups to go to Iraq in violation of U.S. law, live among the people, then return to educate about the death and disease caused by the international sanctions. Kathy and a few other VITW members were in Baghdad when shock and awe struck at the beginning of the war against Iraq in March 2003.

Warning—Danger Ahead

We are painfully conscious not only of how long the course is, but how dangerous. We need to face the sobering reality that running the nonviolent race, mastering the fancy footwork in a confused and jumpy world, is going to create problems. Jesus said, "If the world hates you, keep in mind that it hated me first. If you belonged to the world, it would love you as its own. As it is, you do not belong to the world, but I have chosen you out of the world. That's why the world hates you" (John 15:18-19).

He also said that some of those who reject this way, who support violence when we advocate nonviolence, may be very near to us, even right here: "One's enemies will be the members of one's own household" (Matthew 10:36). The forces who oppose us, whether close at hand or farther away, whether anxious and uncomprehending or callous and cold-blooded, may do us in. The world's hatred can ultimately crucify us, as it did Jesus and Gandhi and Martin Luther King Jr. Leonardo Boff has written, "There are people who are too deeply attached to their quest for wealth and power that leave others out in the cold...Those with power can practice violence to defend themselves. They fashion crosses for those who fight for a world that is less divided between rich and poor. On these crosses they crucify the prophets who proclaim a greater justice, the advocates of the cause of the poor." [1]

Loaves, Fishes, and Teaspoons

Dorothy Day saw hope in our engagement, however small it might be, however unpromising its prospects for success, however isolated we feel in being involved. "What we do is very little. But it is like the little boy with a few loaves and fishes. Christ took that little and increased it. He will do the rest. What we do is so little we may seem to be constantly failing. But so did He fail. He met with apparent failure on the Cross. But unless the seed fall into earth and die, there is no harvest." [2]

Studs Terkel related another image of perseverance, this one given him by Pete Seeger:

Imagine that there's a big seesaw. At one end of it is a basket half full of rocks. That end is on the ground. At the other end is a basket one-quarter full of sand. And a bunch of us with teaspoons, we're trying to put sand in that end. A lot of people laugh at us, they say, "Oh, don't you see, it's leaking out as fast as you're putting it in." Well, we say, "It's leaking out but we're getting more people with teaspoons all the time. One of these days, you're gonna see that whole basket with sand so full that this seesaw is going to go zooooom-up in the other direction." And people will say, "Gee, how did it happen so quickly"? Us and our damned little teaspoons.[3]

Gandhi said that even taking up the nonviolent struggle for justice was a victory of sorts. A nonviolent person always wins something, he believed, even if it's only a strengthening of courage and resolve. We do what we can. We run the race on the course marked out for us by pioneers past and present. We are in joyous kinship with all who have engaged in nonviolent struggle for freedom and justice over the centuries. The New Testament gives us an inspiring image: "Therefore, since we are surrounded by such a great cloud of witnesses, let us throw off everything that hinders us and the sin that so easily enables, and let us run with perseverance the race marked out for us" (Hebrews 12:1).

We receive nourishment from this "cloud of witnesses," strength to carry on, inspiration to stay the course. Let's join that cloud.

Chapter 24

A Different Drumbeat

Daniel Berrigan described the nonviolent approach as "walking to a different drumbeat." The beat, he said, "is complex. It commands fancy footwork...a grander rhythm of conscientious history—a history of sensitivity to the lives, limbs, and spiritual liberty of others." [1]

Berrigan's "grander rhythm of conscientious history" points to the world as it is, and envisions the world as it can become. The world, as it is, is troubled. People are suffering. The "communist enemy" has been replaced with something less tangible and more fearful—terrorism—against which we have begun what may turn out to be George Orwell's perpetual war. Anyone feeling the drumbeat of nonviolence can't help being deeply upset at so many abuses that are so prominent around us. In a world of warring nations, where weapons proliferate, prisoners are tortured, and so much injustice prevails, our reactions of anger and grief—our inward discontent—are natural and healthy.

But we have a vision of what the world can become. For people of faith it's what Jesus described as the Reign of God, where the hungry are fed, the blind see, the lame walk, and everyone has hope. Our spirituality of nonviolence reinforces a longing for that Kindom, a hunger and thirst after justice.

Gandhi advised Jarwaharlal Nehru, India's first Prime Minister shortly after independence from Britain, "Judge every policy on how it will affect the poorest person in the poorest village. If it helps that person it's a good policy. If it doesn't help that person it's not a good policy." We too in our nonviolent spirituality are guided by that same vision of the poorest, the downtrodden, the least powerful. Our vision of peace includes a concern for the well-being of our neighbors everywhere and for the earth itself.

Esoteric Rhythm

The complex drumbeat of nonviolence leads to an unsentimental way of loving difficult people, a realistic way of forgiving those who have trespassed against us. We continue ahead steadfastly, sometimes slowly, occasionally with a burst of joy when a war is stopped, an apartheid transformed, when human rights, civil rights, environmental rights, women's rights are accepted and acclaimed.

Our complex rhythm is out of synch with the mainstream. It's not swaying with the anxious desire to make more money, not sounding the trumpet for honor and glory, not drumming the lust for bending others to our will. It's out of synch in another way also, because it leads us to accept the suffering that is a necessary ingredient of nonviolence. Gandhi believed that the willingness to suffer rather than strike back in retaliation is the key. "Nobody has probably drawn up more petitions or espoused more forlorn causes than I and I have come to this fundamental conclusion that if you want something really important to be done you must not merely satisfy the reason, you must move the heart also. The appeal of reason is more to the head but penetration of the heart comes from suffering. It opens up the inner understanding... Suffering is the badge of the human race, not the sword."[2]

The reign of God may not come in our lifetimes, but we can certainly improve on the present complex. Dom Helder Camara called for "a millennium without misery." Things are better for some, which is proof that they can be better for everyone. Abolition of poverty is a real possibility. A more equitable international economic system can be devised. Torture teams can be disbanded, death squads dissolved, terrorists converted, environmental destruction reversed. Those responsible for provoking terror can be retired from office. The nonviolent person will be impatient—angry in the peace of Christ—until the better world is brought about.

Our esoteric rhythm is the *process* of peace. Nonviolence provides a challenging but satisfying attitude toward life. It calls us beyond being resigned to violence. It offers greater harmony in our relations with others, greater integrity within ourselves, and the sense of being part of a movement to change the world for the better. When we undertake a knowledgeable effort to be nonviolent in all areas of life, marching to that different drumbeat, we become part of a planet-wide movement that can evolve human history to a higher level.

Notes

Chapter 3: Foundations
1. As quoted by Martin Luther King Jr. in "An Experiment in Love." From James M. Washington, ed., *A Testament of Hope: The Essential Writings and Speeches of Martin Luther King Jr.* New York: HarperCollins, 1991, p. 18. (Paperback edition.)
2. Martin Luther King Jr., interview in *Playboy*, January 1965. Reprinted in James M. Washington, ed., *A Testament of Hope: The Essential Writings and Speeches of Martin Luther King Jr.* New York: HarperCollins, 1991, p. 349. (Paperback edition.)

Chapter 4: The Shadow
1. Quoted in Israel Charny, *How Can We Commit the Unthinkable? Genocide: The Human Cancer.* Boulder, CO: Westview Press, 1982, p. 72.

Chapter 6: Stress and Worry
1. Thich Nhat Hanh, *Being Peace.* Berkeley, CA: Parallax Press, 1987, p. 5.

Chapter 9: Nonviolent Leadership
1. One place to find more information about Appreciative Inquiry is http://appreciativeinquiry.cwru.edu/

Chapter 10: Love Not Like
1. See Walter Wink, *The Powers That Be: Theology for a New Millennium.* New York: Galilee Doubleday, 1998, Chapter 5 (Jesus' Third Way).

Chapter 12: Personal Assault
1. As told in Pam McAllister, ed., *Reweaving the Web of Life: Feminism and Nonviolence.* Philadelphia: New Society Publishers, 1982, p. 382.

Chapter 15: Revenge
1. For more information, see Andrew Reding (ed. and translator), *Christianity and Revolution: Thomas Borge's Theology of*

Life. Maryknoll, NY: Orbis Books, 1987.

Chapter 16: Empire
1. Adam Smith, *An Inquiry Into the Nature and Causes of the Wealth of Nations.* First published 1776. From book 4, chapter 7, part 3.
2. Arundhati Roy, "Do Turkeys Enjoy Thanksgiving?" From *The Hindu,* January 18, 2004.

Chapter 17: Group Narcissism: Nationalism
1. Pope Paul VI, *Gaudium et Spes (Pastoral Constitution on the Church in the Modern World).* 1965, Chapter IV, 75.

Chapter 18: The Role of Anger
1. Martin Luther King Jr. interview in *Playboy,* January 1965. Reprinted in James M. Washington, ed., *A Testament of Hope: The Essential Writings and Speeches of Martin Luther King Jr.* New York: HarperCollins, 1991, p. 342. (Paperback edition.)

Part 8: A Nonviolent Vision
1. Leonardo Boff, *Way of the Cross—Way of Justice.* Maryknoll, NY: Orbis Books, 1982, p. 16.

Chapter 22: Sowing Nonviolent Seeds
1. Kenneth W. Morgan, Letter to the *New York Times,* January 30, 1991.
2. David Hartsough, "Faces of Courage and Hope," in *Ground Zero* (newspaper of the Ground Zero community in Bangor, Washington). Winter 1992, p. 7-8.
3. Mahatma Gandhi, *All Men Are Brothers: Life and Thoughts of Mahatma Gandhi as Told in His Own Words.* New York and Paris: Columbia University Press and UNESCO, 1958, p. 87.

Chapter 23: Persevering Witness
1. Leonardo Boff, *Way of the Cross—Way of Justice.* Maryknoll, NY: Orbis Books, 1982, p. 16.
2. Dorothy Day, "Aims and Purposes," February 1940. From Robert Ellsberg, ed., *By Little and By Little: The Selected Writings of Dorothy Day.* New York: Alfred A. Knopf, 1983, p. 92.

3. Studs Turkel, "Hope Dies Last," in *In These Times*, January 2, 2004.

Chapter 24: A Different Drumbeat
1. Daniel Berrigan, *Ten Commandments for the Long Haul*. Nashville: Abington, 1981, p. 100.
2. Mahatma Gandhi, *All Men Are Brothers: Life and Thoughts of Mahatma Gandhi as Told in His Own Words*. New York and Paris: Columbia University Press and UNESCO, 1958, p. 91.

About the author

Pax Christi USA file photo

Gerard Vanderhaar (1931-2005), author of five books on nonviolence as well as numerous articles and other publications, was Professor Emeritus of Religion and Peace Studies at Christian Brothers University in Memphis, Tennessee, where he taught for 28 years. A native of Louisville, Kentucky, he received his doctorate in theology at the University of Saint Thomas (the Angelicum) in Rome. He also taught at the University of Saint John's in New York City, Providence College in Rhode Island, and Wesleyan University in Connecticut. He was a founding member of the Memphis chapter of Pax Christi USA, the Mid-South Peace and Justice Center, and the M.K. Gandhi Institute for Nonviolence. A member of Pax Christi since 1973, he twice chaired its national council. In 1992 he was named a Pax Christi Ambassador of Peace.

Made in the USA
Columbia, SC
03 April 2018